DISCARD

Koehler, Jack H. 1936-
Slingshot shooting
1. Sport 2. Shooting 3. Slingshot I. Title

Published by:

SLING PUBLISHING
N 2689 Spring Lane
Marinette, WI 54143

International Standard Book Number:
0-9765311-0-0 (paper)

1 - 2 - 3 - 4 - 5 - 6 - 7 - 8 - 9
Printed in the United States of America

SLINGSHOT SHOOTING

By

Jack H. Koehler

SLING PUBLISHING
Marinette, WI

ACKNOWLEDGMENTS

A very special thanks to my good friend, and number one editor, John Freckleton. Without his help I would not have been able to complete this book (nor any of my previous books). I would also like to thank Alice Togami, Ernie Warner, and Kay Moreland who have also contributed editing help.

All photographs and illustrations, including the covers, were done by the author.

DEDICATION

This book is dedicated to the slingshot shooters of the world, those of the past, present, and future. And to all the visionaries that perceive a magnificent future for slingshot shooting.

CONTENTS

INTRODUCTION   **1**

1. SAFETY **3**
    SAFETY GLASSES   3
    SHOOTING UP INTO THE AIR   4
    SHOOTING AT BOTTLES   5
    ADOLESCENT SHOOTERS   5
    RICOCHET   6
    CHECK BANDS AND FORKS   6
    SITUATIONAL AWARENESS   6

2. THE SLINGSHOT **9**
    YOKE   10
    WRIST SUPPORT   10
    POWER BANDS   12
        Types
        Stretch and power
        Matching stretch
        Taper
        Flat bands
        Office rubber bands
        Elasticity variables
        Storage
    BAND REPLACEMENT   19
    POUCH   26
        Size

Stiffness
Slipperiness
Width
PROJECTILE VELOCITY   27

3. AMMUNITION **33**
TYPES OF AMMO   33
    Stones
    Marbles
    Lead slugs
    Plastic balls
    Paint balls
    Steel balls
    Alternative ammo
PROJECTILE ENERGY   37
COMPETITION SHOOTING   37

4. SLINGSHOT DESIGN **41**
BUY OR BUILD   41
DESIGN AND CONSTRUCTION ...   42
    Yoke
    Bands
    Pouch
    Attaching bands to fork
    Attaching bands to pouch
TESTING   59

5. TARGET SYSTEMS **61**
SAFETY CONSIDERATIONS   61
    Avoid ricochets
    Errant shots
PRACTICAL SYSTEMS   62

Bull's-eye
Projectile retrieval
Indoor shooting range
ALTERNATIVE RANGES   65
ALTERNATIVE TARGETS   65
     Paint balls
     Plasterboard
     Sand target
     Moving targets

6. HANDEDNESS **69**
     DEFINITION   69
     DOMINANT EYE   69
     STEADIEST HAND   70
     PULLING STRENGTH   71
     LOADING AND HOLDING POUCH   71
     SELECTING THE BEST STANCE ..   72

7. SHOOTING TECHNIQUE ..   **73**
     BODY POSITION   73
        Foot position
        Shoulders
        Arms
        Body
        Head
     THE MECHANICS OF SHOOTING .   77
        Draw length
        Band twist
        Cant angle
        Sling rotation
        Wrist support
        Loading the pouch

Pulling the pouch
Pouch anchor point
Pouch orientation
Pouch release
BREATH CONTROL 91
INTEGRATING SHOT PROCESSES 92

8. AIMING 95
INSTINCTIVE SHOOTING 95
AIMING WITH A SIGHT 97
Move-through technique
Hold-steady technique
AIMING AND TIMING 100
WINDAGE ADJUSTMENTS 101
Projectile speed
Wind speed
Wind direction
Calculating aim corrections
Another aim correction technique

9. MIND AND BODY 107
ROUTINES 107
Physical routines
Mental routines
POSITIVE IMAGING 109
PHYSICAL CONDITIONING 110

10. PRACTICE 113
PRACTICE TIME 113
PRACTICE REGIMEN 115
ACCURACY PLATEAU 116
EQUIPMENT AND ENVIRONMENT .. 116

RECORDS 117
VIDEO REVIEW 118
SELF-COACHING 119
TARGET PANIC 120
ADDRESSING BAD HABITS 121
GOOD DAYS – BAD DAYS 121
THE BASICS 122
HOW GOOD ARE YOU 123

11. TOURNAMENTS 125
TOURNAMENT PROMOTION 125
EQUIPMENT 125
STRESS 127
CHOKING 127
MENTAL PREPAREDNESS 131
Right-brain – left-brain
Imaging
Rehearsals
PHYSICAL PREPAREDNESS 134
Muscle tension
Warm up
Rest and relaxation
Eating
SPONSORSHIP 135
Events
Participants

12. HUNTING 139
SMALL GAME 139
BIG GAME 140
DISTANCE VARIABLES 141
EQUIPMENT 142

Power bands
Ammunition
SAFETY ……………...……………..   144
LEGAL CONSIDERATIONS ………   144

13. EPILOGUE ………....…….......   **147**

ABOUT AUTHOR …………....…….   **149**

INTRODUCTION

There are two basic types of slingshots. The first type is the kind used by David to slay Goliath (in the Biblical story). This type of slingshot consists of a pouch attached to two cords about two to three feet long. A stone, or other type of projectile, is placed in the pouch. The ends of both cords are held in the hand as the pouch is swung in a circular motion to gain momentum. When maximum speed is reached, one of the two cords is released and the projectile goes flying toward the target. A great deal of skill is required to become even minimally proficient with this type of slingshot. This book is **not** about this type of slingshot.

The second type of slingshot (the type that this book is about) consists of a yoke (horns or prongs), handle, and two elastic bands. One end of each band is attached to the fork and the other end to a pouch. A projectile is placed in the pouch; the bands are stretched back, and then released. The projectile is propelled forward between the forks of the yoke by the recoiling bands. This type of slingshot is sometimes referred to as a *"flip"* or *"hand catapult"*. In this book it will be referred to as a *"slingshot"* (not sling shot).

The introduction of the modern slingshot is fairly recent because it requires rubber or other very elastic material for use as bands. Rubber didn't come into wide usage until around 1840; several rubber substitutes were introduced after that time.

Slingshot shooting is a serious activity and is not recommended for unsupervised adolescents. In most states it is illegal for a person under the age of sixteen to buy, shoot, or even possess a slingshot without adult supervision. (Contact your state and local officials for laws pertaining to your specific area.) When used under adult supervision, slingshot shooting is an excellent way to introduce adolescents to the responsibilities involved in all the other types of shooting sports.

This book is geared toward the serious slingshot shooter who's primary objective is tournament competition. This does not mean the "plinker" or "hunter" can't become a much better slingshot shooter by studying this book.

Shooting a slingshot is easy—shooting a slingshot accurately is extremely difficult. It generally takes years of dedicated practice to become an expert slingshot shooter. But, the good thing is that even the learning process will be a pleasurable and rewarding experience.

CHAPTER 1

SAFETY

A slingshot can be a very dangerous device if not given the proper respect. Many people consider a slingshot as being a toy and therefore not dangerous. This kind of thinking makes a slingshot even more dangerous, which can result in catastrophe. Always give the same respect to a slingshot as you would a bow and arrow or gun.

SAFETY GLASSES

There is always a chance that a band could break and possibly recoil back into the eye of the shooter. Therefore, it is strongly recommended that safety glasses always be worn when shooting. Industrial type safety glasses, that can be purchased from hardware stores, are adequate for the casual slingshot shooter. However, those safety glasses were designed for close work like grinding and sawing; therefore, they generally don't have high quality optics. The serious slingshot shooter must be able to see clearly for long distances, which requires high quality optics. Sporting goods stores sell high quality safety glasses used for other types of shooting and therefore they are suitable for slingshot shooting. Be sure the safety glasses do not interfere with your anchor point (Chapter 7) and that they will stay in place, without being too tight, for extended shooting sessions.

When selecting safety glasses there are several things to consider:

1. Some glasses are designed such that the lenses are positioned close to the eyes. This may cause the lens to touch the eye (or eye lash) when the thumb recoils upon releasing the pouch. This little nudge won't cause injury but it may cause a flinch. The flinch will introduce accuracy errors.
2. Some glasses interfere with the anchor point. Do not let the glasses dictate your stance or shooting technique; chose a different style of safety glasses.
3. To avoid distortion, it is important that the line of sight is perpendicular to the lens.
4. If you are a serious tournament competitor, it is advisable to have several pairs of safety glasses, all with a different color or tint, to accommodate different weather and light conditions.

SHOOTING UP INTO THE AIR

Remember that old adage, "What goes up must come down." Shooting up into the air is always dangerous. It may take a little time but the BB (ball bearing) will always come back down, theoretically, at the same speed it went up. This could potentially cause great damage or injury. When shooting up at about 45-degrees the BB will travel the greatest horizontal distance. It is possible for the BB to come down several hundred yards away from where it was released. Therefore, you must always be aware of what could be struck even at a great distances.

SHOOTING AT BOTTLES

Never shoot at glass bottles except in a dump or landfill. Broken glass will remain for centuries and will continue to be a danger to both man and beast. The same danger exists when shooting with glass ammunition (marbles). If the projectile shatters on impact, the hazardous shards will remain behind with the potential of causing injury to someone or something.

ADOLESCENT SHOOTERS

Children and young adults seem to be irresistibly drawn to the thrill of slingshot shooting. However, they are also known to occasionally be irresponsible shooters. If a catastrophe happens to a person, slingshot shooting will become a negative experience. Make every effort to keep slingshot shooting a positive experience by always insisting on responsible adult supervision of adolescents.

The bands on slingshots used by adolescents should be extremely weak. The weak bands will allow the adolescent to develop the proper form (pull and anchor point) without undue strain. And also, the weak bands will insure that the sling won't slip from the sling hand.

Adolescents should be limited to using light Styrofoam BBs. As they become more competent, and responsible, they can advance to using small plastic BBs.

RICOCHET

When hunting or plinking, nearly every shot ricochets off the first object struck and goes on to strike something unintended. Always be aware that this is likely to happen and take the proper precautions.

CHECK BANDS AND FORKS

Always check your equipment before a shooting session. Check for cracks or abrasions on the bands, proper band attachments, and secure pouch attachment. If you take a break from shooting, check your equipment once again before you resume shooting. When you are target shooting the equipment environment is usually controlled, but when you're hunting/plinking the environment is potentially hostile to your equipment. At these times, check your equipment even more frequently.

SITUATIONAL AWARENESS

When target shooting, you generally know where everything and everyone else is located. When hunting/plinking you must constantly be aware of the changing environment. Think before you take the shot. Even if you are standing still, the location of people around you may be constantly changing. As with rifle or shotgun hunting, everyone in the hunting party must know where everyone else is **at all times**.

SLINGSHOT SHOOTING

CHAPTER 2

THE SLINGSHOT

Slingshots come in various sizes and shapes; **figure 2-1** shows a typical commercially manufactured slingshot.

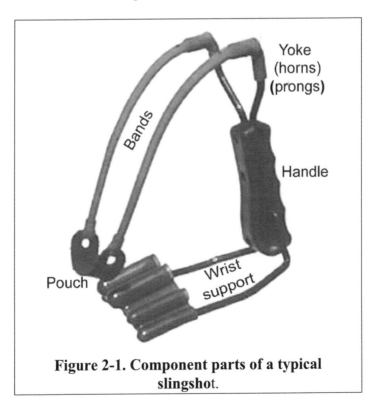

Figure 2-1. Component parts of a typical slingshot.

YOKE

The term *"yoke"* can either refer to the forks (prongs) of a slingshot or the forks and the handle collectively. The forks and handle together are also referred to as a *"sling"*. In the early days, the yoke was commonly made of wood or animal antler, but the modern (commercially available) yoke is generally made out of metal with a plastic handle.

WRIST SUPPORT

The *wrist support* (also referred to as an *arm brace* or *support*) extends back from the yoke and rests on the upper part of the forearm. The wrist support keeps the yoke from tilting backwards when the pouch is pulled to full draw. Not all slingshots are equipped with a wrist support. When bands requiring a low pulling force (weak) are used, the wrist support is not critical; however, if the slingshot has strong bands it is much easier to control the yoke when a wrist support is employed.

There are two popular types of wrist-support designs. In the design shown in **figure 2-2,** the arm must be threaded through the support before grasping the slingshot handle. The advantage of this design is that the sling handle can be release and used to aid in loading the pouch. The entire slingshot hangs on the wrist during the loading process. This design is best suited to shooters that, for any reason, have trouble grasping the handle. Another advantage of this design is that the handle can be held loosely while still maintaining control of the slingshot. Being able to hold the handle loosely helps prevent one fork from being rotated ahead of the other.

The other design, shown in **figure 2-3,** allows the handle to be grasped from below the support. This design is more popular because it is considered easier to use.

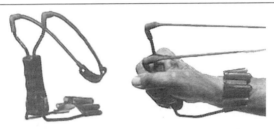

Figure 2-2. The hand must be threaded up through the wrist support before grasping the handle.

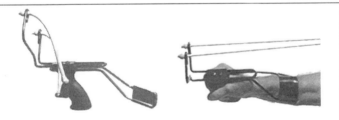

Figure 2-3. The wrist support extends from the upper part of the slingshot.

The wrist support should be adjusted (bent) to fit the individual user—an ill-fitting wrist support is of little functional value.

POWER BANDS

Types -- There are two types of power bands in wide usage—**flat** bands and **tubular** bands. Both types are generally made of surgical latex rubber and are normally 8- to 10-inches long. Flat bands are not as common as the tubular bands because they are not readily available commercially. Most commercially available slingshots come with tubular-type power bands. The tubular bands are about $\frac{1}{4}$- to $\frac{3}{8}$-inch outside diameter with a $\frac{1}{8}$-inch inside diameter.

Stretch and power -- It is imperative that the stretch and power of the bands be suited to the individual using the slingshot. It is desirable to use strong, fast bands so that the projectile travels at a high velocity and therefore drops less on its way to the target. Also, a fast projectile won't be affected by wind as much as a slower one. Weak bands can be held steadier than strong bands, therefore, if the bands require too much pulling force (for a particular shooter) it will be difficult to hold the slingshot steady enough for accurate shooting. A compromise must be made, use the strongest bands you can handle without being unsteady.

Power bands from different suppliers vary somewhat in pull force. If you are not familiar with the stretch and power characteristics of a particular brand of band, you won't know what you are getting until you install them on your slingshot. When you find a brand that has the characteristics you desire, stick with that brand.

All bands have a problem with a phenomenon called *hysteresis*. Hysteresis literally means, "to lag behind". In reference to slingshot bands, hysteresis means the bands are slow to react. That is, the projectile is long gone before the band has finished contracting. Obviously, this means a loss of energy, or simply *inefficiency*. The hysteresis problem varies depending on the weight of the projectile. The greater the weight of the projectile, the less hysteresis effects efficiency.

It should be noted that just because a band is hard to pull does not necessarily mean that it will propel a BB faster than a weaker band. Think of it this way; there is a maximum speed that any particular band will retract (influences speed of projectile). If you put two or three similar bands side by side, the force required to pull them back will increase but the retraction speed (speed of projectile) will remain the same. The multiple bands will, however, be able to propel a large, heavy projectile, as fast, or nearly as fast, as a light one. Obviously, for greatest efficiency (least pulling force for greatest projectile speed), the band characteristics must be matched to the weight of the projectile. **Table 2-1** shows the pull required for several different bands and the resulting speed (measured with a chronograph) of three different sized BBs.

BAND	PULL (Lbs)	SPEED in Feet/Sec		
		$\frac{1}{4}$" BB	$\frac{3}{8}$" BB	$\frac{1}{2}$" BB
A - Flat thick	18.8	148	142	130
B - Tubular	17.2	146	141	131
C - Flat double	13.5	189	172	153
D - Flat single	7.0	161	142	117

Table 2-1. Band "A" was flat, $^{13}/_{16}$-inch wide and $^{1}/_{16}$-inch thick. Band "B" was tubular with $^{11}/_{32}$-inch outside diameter and $^{7}/_{32}$-inch inside diameter. Band "C" was flat $^{1}/_{32}$-inch thick and tapered from $^{3}/_{4}$-inch wide at the fork to $^{9}/_{16}$-inch wide at the pouch with two bands per side. Band "D" was the same as "C" but with only one band on each side.

Matching stretch -- In order for a slingshot to shoot accurately, both bands must recoil with the same force and speed. This is particularly important for slingshot competition where accuracy is paramount. To test a pair of bands, on a slingshot, put a roller **(figure 2-4),** or some other type of small pulley, in the pouch and pull it back to full draw. If the roller turns, as tension is applied to the bands, the bands are unequal. There is nothing you can do to remedy the problem of unmatched bands—they must be replaced.

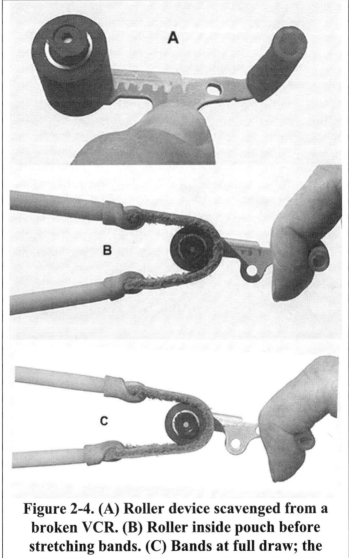

Figure 2-4. (A) Roller device scavenged from a broken VCR. (B) Roller inside pouch before stretching bands. (C) Bands at full draw; the roller has turned because the bottom band is stronger than the upper band.

Taper -- Some bands are wide (or thick) at the fork and become smaller toward the pouch. Tapered bands are generally more efficient than bands that are not tapered. Band efficiency is the relationship between the velocity of the projectile and the pull force required to produce that velocity. (The efficiency of an individual set of bands can vary depending on the weight of the projectile.)

Flat bands -- Flat bands are usually about 0.5-inch wide and a little less than 0.1-inch thick. In the early days of slingshot shooting all bands were flat. This is because they were made out of readily available discarded rubber inner-tubes (the tubes use to be installed inside automobile tires). Nowadays, it is almost as hard to find a rubber inner-tube as it is to find a commercially available flat slingshot band.

In recent years, extremely thin (about 0.03 inch) flat bands have become common for competition shooting. These bands deliver high projectile speeds with a relatively small pull force.

Office rubber bands -- Rubber bands that are available from office-supply stores can be used as slingshot power bands. The rubber bands can be tied (looped) together end to end until the desired length is attained. Either the number 64 ($^1/_4$-inch wide) or the number 84 ($^1/_2$-inch wide) bands can be used **(figure 2-5)**. Several bands can be tied together side-by-side or end-to-end to make the slingshot band longer and/or stronger. Some shooters like to use the wider number 84 bands near the fork and the narrower number 64 bands near the pouch to simulate a tapered band.

Figure 2-5. The bands for this slingshot were purchased from an office-supply store.

Elasticity variables -- There are several variables that affect band elasticity, which subsequently affects projectile speed.

Brand new bands do not stretch and retract consistently the first few times they are used. For this reason, new bands should be broken-in by stretching them six or eight times before the slingshot is used. Even bands that have been broken-in should be pre-stretched a few times before doing any serious shooting.

When pre-stretching bands, pull the pouch back and continue holding it as the tension is taken off. Releasing an empty pouch, from full draw, will cause undue stress on the bands.

If the pouch is held at full draw for a long period of time, the bands will lose some elasticity (speed) when the pouch is released. For maximum accuracy (uniformity) the holding time should be about the same for each shot.

Ambient temperature will also affect the elasticity of the bands. For maximum accuracy the bands must be kept at a uniform temperature during the shooting session. Do not expose the bands to direct sunlight for long periods of time, the heat and ultraviolet rays will alter streachability and ultimately damage the bands.

Storage -- Always store a slingshot such that the bands are straight but not stretched. Any bend in the stored bands will have a tendency to *set*. If your replacement bands come bent up in a package, they should be taken out and stored straight for a period of time before being installed on the slingshot. For longest life, bands should be stored in a cool, dry, dark environment. Even when stored properly, bands will deteriorate over time.

BAND REPLACEMENT

All power bands deteriorate; they develop cracks, break, discolor, and lose elasticity over time. How long the bands last depends on their use. A band that is stretched a few inches more than another (due to shooting stance) will deteriorate faster. Storage and exposure to chemicals will also affect band life. When you detect an errant shot that is obviously not due to aim error, check the bands for tears, slippage, etc before shooting another shot. This inspection may save you from being snapped in the face by a broken band during the next shot.

Eventually, all bands will have to be replaced. When replacing tubular bands do as follows:

1. Remove the old band by rolling it off the fork as shown in **figure 2-6**.

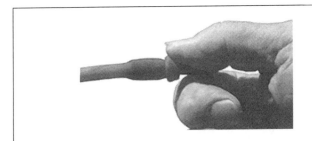

Figure 2-6. Remove the old band by rolling it off the fork with the thumb.

2. If the end adaptors are tight and free of cracks leave them on; otherwise, force off the old adaptors.

3. Clean the ends of each fork with alcohol and let dry thoroughly.

4. Press on the plastic end adaptors (supplied with the bands) onto each fork **(figure 2-7)**.

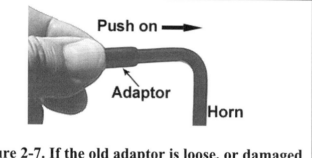

Push on ➡

Adaptor

Horn

Figure 2-7. If the old adaptor is loose, or damaged in any way, cut it off and replace it with a new one.

5. Be sure that both bands are the same length. If they aren't, cut the end off the longest one with a pair of sharp scissors.

6. Place the bands side by side on a flat surface with the apex of the pouch vertical.

7. Mark the top of both bands **(figure 2-8)** with a felt-tip pen so that the pouch will be properly orientated after installation.

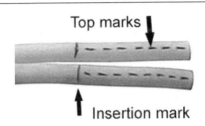

Top marks

Insertion mark

Figure 2-8. Mark the bands on top and at the point where the end of the horn should be when it is fully inserted (insertion mark).

8. Mark the band to indicate where the end of the horn will be when inserted **(figure 2-9)**. Without the mark, one band may be stretched on (rather than slid on) greater than the other making the effective stretchable portion unequal in length.

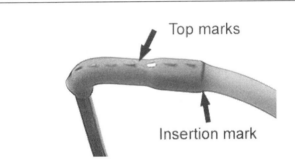

Top marks

Insertion mark

Figure 2-9. Be sure the top marks and the insertion mark are in the proper position after the band has been pressed on.

9. To avoid leaving compressed air inside the band, clamp off a section (the length of the insertion) of

the band (see **figure 2-10**). After the band has been slid onto the horn, the clamp can be released.

Figure 2-10. Air pressure builds inside the tubing as it is forced onto the horn. A clamp is placed on the tubing before inserting it on the horn. When the clamp is released the air pressure subsides.

10. Submerge the tip of the band about $\frac{1}{8}$-inch into rubbing alcohol. Squeeze and release the band causing the alcohol to be sucked up inside the band. Remove the band from the alcohol and squeeze again to remove the excess alcohol from inside the band.

The alcohol makes the band slippery so that it will slip onto the fork easier. It is important to keep the fingers free of alcohol so the band won't slip, in the hand, when forcing it onto the fork.

11. Moisten the end of the horn and adaptor with alcohol. While the fork is still moist, quickly force the moistened band onto the fork. The end of the band should be forced a minimum of about $\frac{1}{2}$-inch past the adaptor. Be sure to keep the marks on the band centered on the top of the fork.

> If the alcohol evaporates before the band is in the proper position, you will have to remove the band and start all over again.

12. Follow the same procedure to install the other band.
13. Set the slingshot aside for 24 hours before stretching the bands or shooting the slingshot.

> There are times when you must use the slingshot immediately after replacing the bands. Here is what I do in those cases: Slip the band a little farther onto the fork (about an inch past the plastic adaptor). After allowing the alcohol to dry for a few minutes, roll the band back off the fork about $1/4$-inch (**figure 2-11**). Wipe the band and horn so they are clean and free of alcohol. Put contact cement on both the sling horn and band. Let it dry until it isn't sticky to the touch then roll the band back onto the horn.

Figure 2-11. Contact cement can be used to insure that the band does not slip off the fork.

Figures 2-12 to **2-15** show some errors to avoid when replacing bands.

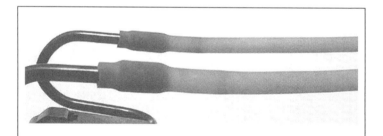

Figure 2-12. Bands have not been inserted far enough onto the forks.

Figure 2-13. Uneven insertion, the lower band will pull harder than the top band.

Figure 2-14. The bottom of the bottom band is stretched on farther than the top causing a bend in the band at the adaptor.

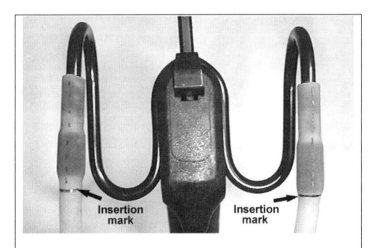

Figure 2-15. The ends of both bands have been inserted an equal distance onto the forks. However, the band on the left has been stretched on as evidenced by the uneven insertion marks.

POUCH

Size -- Ideally, the pouch should be as small as possible while still being functional. An excessively large pouch will be heavy and thus inhibit the acceleration of the pouch as it is released. A large pouch will add aerodynamic drag, which also slows down the pouch and projectile.

Stiffness -- The pouch is generally made of leather. Some pouches are extremely stiff; this makes it difficult to keep the BB centered in the pouch. But, the advantage of a stiff pouch is that both sides of the pouch will slip through the fingers at the same time (one side won't precede the other) when released. When using a soft pliable pouch, uneven release may be a problem.

Slipperiness -- If the pouch is too smooth it may be hard to hold in the full draw position. The stronger the bands, the more difficult it is to hold. Another problem is that when the pouch is released, one side of a smooth pouch may slip forward before the other, this causes the BB to fly off course. To alleviate the slipperiness, roughen the outer surface of the pouch with sandpaper.

Width -- An extremely wide pouch is difficult to load properly because the BB does not stay centered in the pouch. A wide pouch can be made thinner by trimming it with a razorblade or similar sharp cutting instrument. Be sure not to remove any leather from the part of the pouch that attaches to the band, which would reduce its strength. Keep in mind that the pouch can reach speeds up to of 200 mph; a wide pouch will create considerable aerodynamic drag at that speed. The drag will slow it down, which translates to a loss of power. Another potential problem with a wide pouch is *flutter* (like a flag blowing in the wind). If the pouch starts to flutter, before the BB is released, it will throw the projectile off course. Generally, a big or stiff pouch will not release the BB the same way each shot. This causes small errors on each shot and occasionally a huge error. When a slingshot does not shoot as consistently as you expect, suspect a faulty pouch.

PROJECTILE VELOCITY

It is nice to know the velocity of the projectile when using different slingshots, different bands, or different types of ammo. Velocity can be measured very accurately with an instrument called a *chronograph*. Chronographs cost about a hundred dollars, or more, so not everyone will see fit to invest in one. An alternative solution would be to go to a gun club, paint-ball club, or archery club, and ask to use their chronograph. If you offer a few dollars rental fee, they may be happy to let you use their equipment.

Short of using a chronograph, to determine velocity, there are ways of determining relative velocity. For example, you may want to know which of two slingshots shoots faster or which of two sets of bands propel the projectile faster. These comparisons can be determined without the use of a chronograph.

To determine which of two slingshots propels a BB at a higher velocity do the following: Set the sight of each slingshot at a target 10-meters away. Then, with each slingshot, aim and shoot the exact same way when shooting at a target 20-meters away. The BB that drops the most, when shooting at the 20-meter target, indicates the slower slingshot.

To determine which of two sets of power bands propels a BB faster do this: Set the sight of a slingshot, with one set of bands, at a target 20-meters away. Then, replace the bands and aim the exact same way at the target. If the BB strikes the target higher, the velocity is faster than the old band—if it strikes the target lower, the velocity is slower.

For those of you that are technically inclined, there is way to determine the velocity of a projectile without using a chronograph: The technique requires shooting a shot while the bands are held precisely horizontal (level). Determine a way of holding a "bubble-level" adjacent to the bands while shooting. Mark the point where the level is pointing on a target 10-meters away. Keep the bands aligned with the adjacent bubble-level and shoot a shot at the target. It is best to hold the slingshot vertically (no cant angle) when shooting this shot. Measure the distance the BB dropped below the level mark on the target.

To obtain travel time; calculate 2 times the distance dropped divided by 32. Then, find the square root of the result to determine travel time. Divide the distance to the target by travel time to get average velocity.

For example: Assume the BB dropped 1.2 feet in 32.8 feet (10 meters).

(2 x 1.2) / 32 = 0.075

Using a calculator we determine the square root of 0.075 is 0.274 (travel time). Therefore, the time required for the BB to get to the target is **0.274 seconds**.

Velocity equals distance to the target divided by travel time.

32.8 / 0.274 = 120

Therefore, the average velocity of the projectile, from the slingshot to the target, was **120 feet per second**.

If you don't want to bother doing the math, you can use **table 2-1** to determine projectile velocity.

Drop (in feet)	Feet Per Second	Miles Per Hour
0.1	415	283
.2	293	200
.3	240	163
.4	207	141
.5	186	126
.6	169	115
.7	157	107
.8	147	100
.9	138	94
1.0	131	89
1.1	125	85
1.2	120	82
1.3	115	78
1.4	111	76
1.5	107	73
1.6	104	71
1.7	101	69
1.8	98	67
1.9	95	65
2.0	93	63
2.1	90	62
2.2	88	60
2.3	86	59
2.4	85	58
2.5	83	56

Table 2-1. Assuming the projectile is shot level, the measured drop, in a distance of 10 meters, can be converted to velocity.

Conversion factors:

Multiply **Feet per Second** by 0.682 to get **MPH**

Multiply **MPH** by 1.47 to get **Feet per Second**.

SLINGSHOT SHOOTING

CHAPTER 3

AMMUNITION

Common names for slingshot ammunition include:

Slug - Works well for a metal ball but doesn't quite fit when using a stone or glass marble as ammunition.

Pellet - We usually think of a pellet as being a cylindrical not spherical.

Projectile - Works well for all types of ammo including stones and arrows.

BB - Short for "*ball bearing*" but may be mistaken for the BBs used in a BB gun, which are very small.

Use whatever term you like but be aware of its connotation. In this book "BB" and "projectile" are used most of the time.

TYPES OF AMMO

Stones -- In the past, stones were the most common type of ammo used for slingshots. The most compelling reasons to use stones is that they are inexpensive and usually readily available. The problem with stones is that they provide limited accuracy. All stones are a little different in size, weight, sphericity, and surface roughness. Each of these characteristics influence its flight path. If accuracy is not important, stones are still a good choice for ammunition.

Marbles -- In the past, glass marbles were sometimes used (as a substitute for stones) when increased accuracy was desired. The price of glass marbles increased for many years making them very expensive for use as slingshot ammo. However, recently the price of marbles has come down considerably making them, once again, a viable option. The down side of using glass marbles is that they shatter into shards when they strike something solid like a rock. These glass shards can be dangerous and, they remain dangerous forever (glass is not biodegradable). Shards accumulate on the ground around favored targets because they are nearly impossible to clean up. This means that the danger of being impaled, by a shard of glass, reminds indefinitely.

One advantage of using marbles, especially the transparent ones, is that their trajectory can usually be seen (because of refracted light). This is an advantage for all shooters and especially for those that shoot (aim) instinctively.

Lead slugs -- Lead slugs of various sizes are sometimes used as slingshot ammo. Lead is denser than other types of ammo; therefore, the projectiles can be smaller for a given weight. This means that a lead ball will experience less air resistance, and consequently fly faster, than a comparable weight slug made of a less dense material.

34

Lead slugs can be purchased at sporting goods stores that cater to firearm reloaders. Double-ought Buckshot can be used as small projectiles, and muzzle-loading slugs can be used as larger ammo. If you insist on using lead slugs, you should consider casting your own like serious firearm shooters do.

Even though lead slugs have some advantages, they are not recommended for use as slingshot ammo because of environmental concerns. Handling lead can be hazardous to your health. Lead residue can get onto your hands and from there into your mouth; ingesting lead has been proven to be harmful. Also, game animals could eat the scattered lead shot and consequently past on the harmful effects to whomever eats these animals.

Plastic balls -- Plastic balls, made for a variety of purposes, can be used as slingshot ammo. Plastic balls made for *airsoft* guns are suitable for plinking purposes, however, they are on the small side (6mm) and are fairly light (0.12 to 0.25 grams). But, they make attractive slingshot ammunition because they are inexpensive.

Some vendors sell $^1/_2$-inch diameter white, plastic balls as slingshot ammo. Their white color makes their trajectory easier to see than most other ammo especially for the longer shots.

Paint balls -- Commercially available paint balls are fun to use as ammunition under certain circumstances. The standard sized paint ball is a little large (0.68-inch diameter) for slingshot usage. However, special purpose paint balls are available in $^1/_2$-inch and 6-mm sizes. The $^1/_2$-inch balls are ideal for slingshot usage. Paint balls leave behind a mess (although temporary) so be careful how and when you use them.

Steel balls -- The most common type of slingshot ammo is the steel ball. Steel balls are usually rejects from the manufacture of ball bearings (hence the term "BB") for industrial purposes. The most commonly used sizes are $^1/_4$-, $^5/_{16}$-, $^3/_8$-, and $^1/_2$-inch diameters.

The $^1/_4$-inch BBs are usually used for plinking (unretrieved) because they are relatively inexpensive. The $^3/_8$-inch BBs are the most commonly used size for competition shooting and therefore for target practice as well. The cost of $^3/_8$-inch BBs is not a primary consideration because they are usually retrieved and used over and over again. The $^1/_2$-inch steel BBs are usually used for hunting small game and varmints. They have more mass than the smaller BBs and therefore have a greater stopping power.

Alternative ammo -- *Arrows* can be used (with a modified slingshot) for small game, fish, amphibians, and other types of critters. *Sand* (requires a special type of pouch) can be used for sport hunting of wasps, hornets, bees, and other types of pests. *Fine shot* (used in certain shotgun shells) and BBs made for BB guns can be used for shooting ping pong balls out of the air and other types of fun target shooting.

> Caution: Be extra careful when using any kind of alternative ammo, there is a heightened chance that something may go wrong and an accident could happen. Be especially careful when using extra small BBs, they frequently slip out of the pouch prematurely and strike the shooter in the sling hand.

PROJECTILE ENERGY

The energy of a projectile is determined by its weight and velocity. The greater the weight and/or velocity, the greater the energy. However, air resistance starts robbing the projectile of its energy as soon as it leaves the pouch. Air resistance increases exponentially with a projectile's speed. This means fast projectiles lose energy more rapidly than slower projectiles. In fact, fast, light projectiles lose energy so rapidly that after 10 meters or so they can be traveling slower than heavy projectiles that were released at a slower initial speed. This is generally not important when shooting at a target 10-meters away. But, it does become a significant factor when shooting at longer distances, or when hunting where projectile energy is a major consideration.

COMPETITION SHOOTING

In competition shooting you must use the best ammo available. If you miss the bull's-eye you don't want it to be because of a flaw in the BB. The BBs used as slingshot ammo are usually seconds or rejects from the manufacturer of industrial ball bearings. As such, they have some type of imperfection. These imperfections cause the ball to fly slightly off-course.

Obviously, the best way to get ball bearings that don't have imperfections is to purchase "perfect" ball bearings directly from the factory. Unfortunately, that option isn't available to most of us because of the high cost (about ten times more expensive than flawed BBs). The next best option is to buy high grade slingshot BBs then inspect them for flaws and categorize them.

Some vendors deal exclusively with BBs that have a small flat spot on their surface, these BBs are adequate for everything except competition shooting. Other vendors sell BBs that are not matched in size or are out-of-round (not spherical). It is best to start with these BBs and sort them into size categories. You could check each one with a micrometer but that would take considerable time and patients. **Figure 3-1** shows an apparatus I built to help facilitate the sorting process.

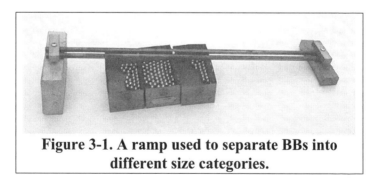

Figure 3-1. A ramp used to separate BBs into different size categories.

To fabricate a BB sorter, position two steel rods parallel to each other and separated a little less than the diameter of the balls to be tested. Then, increase the separation at one end so that the rods are a little more than a ball's width apart. Lastly, lower the wide end so that a BB set on the small end will roll towards the big end and, at some point, fall between the rods. The larger the BB the farther down the rods it will travel before falling. Separate the BBs into two or three size categories. Keep in mind, it is not the absolute size of the BB that is important, it's uniformity. Once you set your slingshot sight for a particular size BB, you must compete with that same size BB. If you change ammo size you must reset the sight or compensate with aim (the larger BBs will strike lower on the target).

If a BB is out-of-round (not spherical) it may curve on the way to the target. To check for sphericity run the size-sorted BBs through the test (with the rods) several more times. Those that are not spherical will not fall in the same place every time.

After the BBs have been sorted by size, and checked for sphericity, they must be checked for surface irregularities. Any little pit may cause the BB to curve unpredictably on its way to the target. BBs with rust spots or scratches should not be used for serious competition.

SLINGSHOT SHOOTING

CHAPTER 4

SLINGSHOT DESIGN

BUY OR BUILD

Inevitably, everyone will have to answer the question of whether to buy or build his or her own slingshot. When I was a kid we had no choice, there were no commercially available slingshots (at least that I was aware of) so I had to build my own. It's a different story nowadays, factory made slingshot are available from many sources. Factory made slingshots are inexpensive, and in some ways, superior to the homemade types. So why would anyone want to build a slingshot? The answer is— some people find the building challenging and, the final product, gratifying.

In the following discussion I will explain how, in the past, common slingshots were built. For legal reasons, I do not advocate building your own slingshot nor do I consider the designs presented here as being safe or reliable. If you decide to build your own slingshot, do whatever is necessary to assure that it is safe; the liability is yours.

DESIGN AND CONSTRUCTION

Here, we will present the design and construction of simple basic designs and also some design variations. Ambitious builders may want to add wrist braces, sights, and/or vibration dampeners, as they deem necessary. Once the basic slingshot is constructed, it is an easy matter to alter the design to incorporate individual preferences.

At any national tournament, it is difficult to find any two shooters using identical slingshots. Obviously, all the top shooters have their own ideas about ideal slingshot design.

Yoke -- The yoke (sling or fork) of a homemade slingshot was usually made of wood, although deer antlers, metal, and other material had been employed. When using wood, there is a choice between cutting a fork from a piece of flat stock or finding a branch, from a tree, that is already in the shape of a fork.

Figure 4-1 a shows several forks cut from trees in my back yard. Generally, there should be between 3 and 4 inches between the ends of the fork. (Some prefer shorter, narrower forks; it is mostly personal preference.) The forks must be cut and trimmed to the desired size and the bark removed (if left on, the bark accelerates wood decay).

Figure 4-1. Several tree branches that will eventually become slingshots.

Figure 4-2 shows four wooden forks ready for band installation. When the fork is cut from a board, it is essential that a sturdy board (usually hardwood) be used and that the grain is in the direction of the forks (vertical).

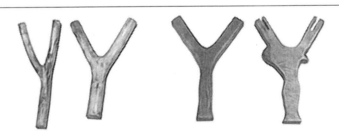

Figure 4-2. The two forks on the left were made from tree branches and the two on the right were cut from a maple board.

Bands -- In the olden days bands were cut from discarded inner-tubes that came from inside automobile tires. Since the advent of tubeless tires, inner-tubes are no longer a plentiful source for band material. However, there are still some tires that use inner-tubes: motorcycles and farm-implement tires are examples.

Assuming an inner-tube was used: Two strips of rubber about $1/2$-inch wide and about 10-inches long were cut from the tube. The width and length varied depending on individual preference (pull force and pull length).

Nowadays, commercial slingshot replacement bands (latex tubing) are readily available from internet vendors, from sporting goods stores, or from department stores that have a sporting goods department (like Wal Mart). An advantage of using commercially available replacement bands is that the pouch is already attached to the bands. Another source of band material is rubber bands from office-supply stores. The large bands (#64 or #84) can be tied together side by side and/or end-to-end to produce almost any length and desired pull force.

Pouch -- If the pouch is not already attached to the bands when purchased, it must be fabricated from scratch. The pouch is made from any suitable leather source such as a belt or a discarded pair of leather shoes. If the leather on the main body of the shoe is too thick, the tongue leather is used. The pouch material must be thick enough, and strong enough, to hold together when subjected to the tension of the bands at full draw.

To fabricate a pouch, a rectangular piece of leather about $3/4$-inch wide and 3-inches long is used (wider and longer if large ammo was used). A hole about $1/4$-inch in diameter is punched or drilled about $3/8$-inch from each end of the pouch as shown in **figure 4-3.**

The hole in the leather pouch can be made with a drill if it is clamped between two pieces of wood. Or, it can be punched out using a paper-binder hole punch.

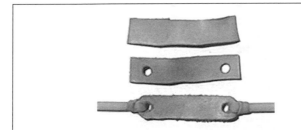

Figure 4-3. Three stages in the fabrication of a leather pouch.

Attaching bands to fork -- There are several different ways the bands can be attached to the fork. The most common way is shown in **figure 4-4**. A notch is carved around the circumference of the horn about $\frac{1}{2}$-inch from the end. The band is stretch over the end of the horn, while the band is stretched; a string (or rubber strap) is wrapped tightly around the band, at the notch, and tied off. It is tempting to use wire to fasten the bands to the forks. However, it is best never to use anything that may come loose and recoil back into the eye or face of the shooter.

With the tying technique shown in **figures 4-4** "**A**" and "**B**", the tie string tends to cut into the band, when at full draw, and cause band failure. The tying technique shown in "**C**" (band secured to only the front side of the horn) minimizes this problem. The downside of using this tying technique is that the band must be carefully positioned over the center of the horn before each shot.

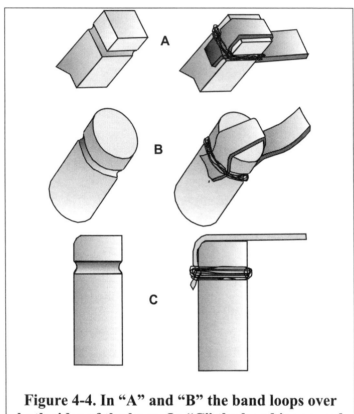

Figure 4-4. In "A" and "B" the band loops over both sides of the horn. In "C" the band is secured only to the front side of the horn.

Another common attachment technique is shown in **figure 4-5**. In this system, two slots are sawed in the tip of the each fork. The width of the slot depends on the type of band that is used. If flat bands are used the slots are made a little less than one half the thickness of the band. If tubular bands are used the width of the slots are made about one fourth the diameter of the band.

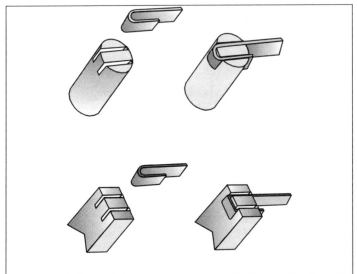

Figure 4-5. In this attachment technique, the band is threaded around a tenon in the horn.

To install, the end of the band is held and stretched so that it becomes thinner. It is then slid into one of the slots. The band is pulled until there is about $\frac{1}{4}$-inch of band sticking out from the slot. Then, it is looped back around the tenon and inserted in the other slot going in the opposite direction (toward shooter). When using a slingshot with this type of band attachment, always check to be sure the bands have not moved in the slot.

Figure 4-6 shows how tubular bands are attached to a metal horn.

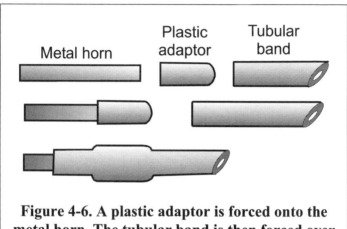

Figure 4-6. A plastic adaptor is forced onto the metal horn. The tubular band is then forced over the adaptor and onto the metal horn.

Figures 4-7 to **4-10** show some other, less common, techniques for attaching bands to forks.

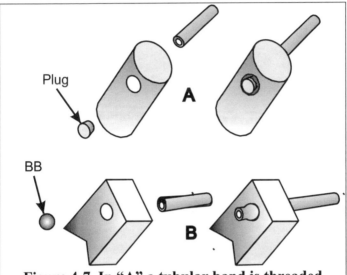

Figure 4-7. In "A" a tubular band is threaded through a hole in the horn and wedge-shaped plug is inserted into the band. In "B" instead of a wedge-shaped plug, a BB is inserted into the tubular band.

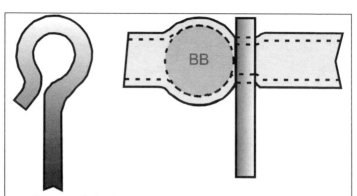

Figure 4-8. A BB is inserted into the end of a tubular band. The band is then stretched and inserted into a hook in a metal fork.

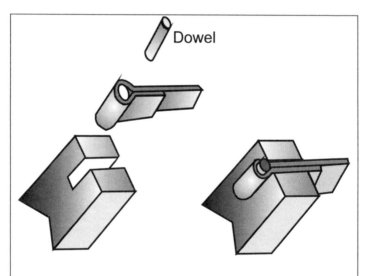

Figure 4-9. The band is threaded through a slot in the horn, around a wooden dowel, then back through the slot.

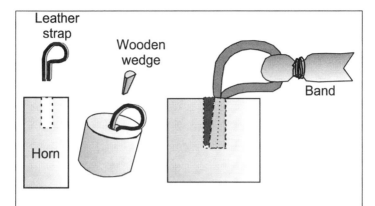

Leather strap

Wooden wedge

Band

Horn

Figure 4-10. This attachment technique is popular in Europe. A leather strap is wedged into a hole in the end of the horn. The band is then attached to the leather strap.

It would be easy to attach the bands to the forks using metal bolts, screws, or clamps. These attachment techniques must be avoided because of safety concerns. It must always be assumed that the attachment apparatus will, at some time in the future, break off and snap back into the shooters face.

Attaching bands to pouch -- Figure 4-11 shows the most common way of attaching the bands (flat or tubular) to the pouch. The band is threaded through the hole in the pouch from the inside to the outside. (If threaded in the opposite direction, the end of the band may push the BB off course.) After passing through the hole in the pouch, the band is folded back, stretched, then tied with string. (I personally prefer to use coarse elastic thread rather than string to secure the bands to the pouch because it expands and contracts along with the band.)

51

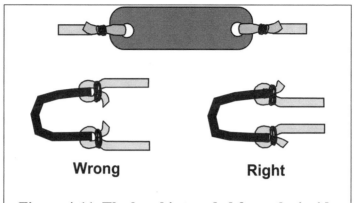

Figure 4-11. The band is treaded from the inside out, then tied with string.

The attachment technique shown graphically in **figure 4-12** utilizes a portion of tubing, instead of a string, to secure the band to the pouch.

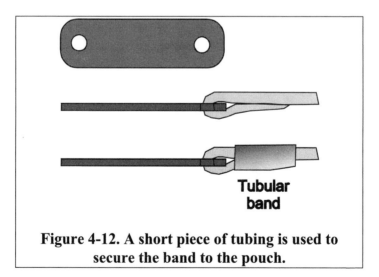

Figure 4-12. A short piece of tubing is used to secure the band to the pouch.

Figures 4-13 A through **D** show how the band type of attachment is fabricated. A pair of needle-nosed pliers is used to stretch open the tie tubing. (Before using the pliers it is best to file off the gripping serrations inside the jaws.) Use a block of wood, placed inside the handles of the pliers, to hold the jaws open while positioning the tie band. Moistening the pliers and tubing with rubbing alcohol helps keep the parts slippery.

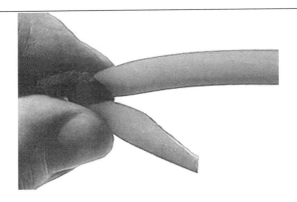

Figure 4-13 A. The end of the band is cut at an angle.

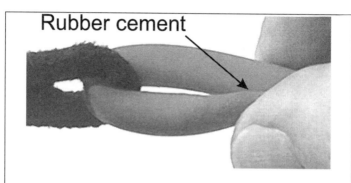

Rubber cement

Figure 4-13 B. The band is threaded through the hole in the pouch. Rubber cement is used to maintain the loop during fabrication.

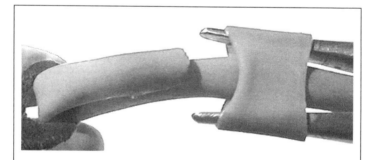

Figure 4-13 C. A small portion of band is spread with a needle-nosed pliers and slipped onto the looped end of the band.

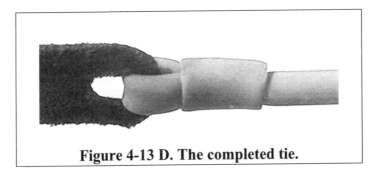

Figure 4-13 D. The completed tie.

When using commercially purchased replacement bands, the pouch is usually already attached. The commercial type of attachment system is shown in **figure 4-14**.

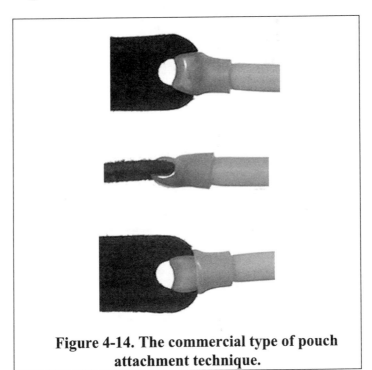

Figure 4-14. The commercial type of pouch attachment technique.

The commercial type of attachment system can be duplicated using the technique shown in **figures 4-15 A** through **D**.

Figure 4-15 A. A hole is burned into the band with a red-hot $^{3}/_{32}$-inch diameter nail or similar type of metal rod. (The tubing is pressed onto a jaw of a needle-nosed pliers to prevent the hole from going through both sides of the tubing.)

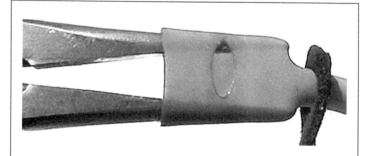

Figure 4-15 B. The tubing is threaded through the hole in the pouch. The end of the band is spread using a pair of needle-nosed pliers.

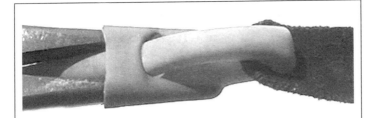

Figure 4-15 C. The tubing is threaded back through the hole and out the end.

Figure 4-15 D. The tubing is pulled tight around the pouch.

This type of pouch attachment is great for a commercial product because it can be done with a machine. However, there is a problem. As the band is pulled to full draw, the attachment squeezes the pouch tighter and tighter as shown in **figure 4-16 A**. This causes a bend in the end of the pouch as shown in **figure 4-17**. The bend causes the pouch to veer off course when it is released because of the aerodynamics. When this happens, the shot will be extremely inaccurate.

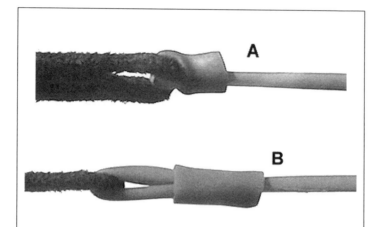

Figure 4-16. In "A", the pouch is squeezed because the attachment becomes increasingly tighter as the band is stretched. In "B" the pouch attachment does not pull tighter as the band is stretched.

Figure 4-17. The end of the pouch is bent due to the squeezing of the attachment band. In this condition, I would not dare to shoot with this slingshot. The pouch could get tangled up with the BB and cause the BB to strike the sling hand.

TESTING

Before using a new slingshot, it should be tested for safety and accuracy. To perform the safety test, hold the pouch and stretch the bands back while holding it away from your face. Stretch it and let it slowly retract; repeat this exercise but each time stretch the bands a little farther. If it can be stretched greater than that required for your normal shooting stance, without breaking, you could start using it for shooting.

All new slingshots shoot a little differently; therefore, they must be tested for accuracy. When testing, brace your sling hand on something solid like a door jam or fence post. This will insure that any inaccuracy will be caused by the slingshot and not from unsteadiness. Shoot several shots at different distances and with different size ammo.

If you are use to shooting a slingshot that has a wrist support, and your new slingshot does not have one, you will have to learn a new shooting technique. To keep the top of the slingshot from tilting back, as the pouch is being pulled, you must brace the sling with your thumb and fore finger as shown in **figure 4-18**.

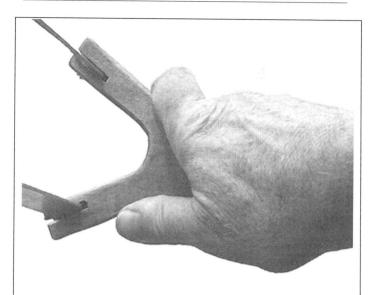

Figure 4-18. If the slingshot doesn't have a wrist support, the fingers must be moved up onto the forks for stability.

CHAPTER 5

TARGET
SYSTEMS

Some people use their slingshots for plinking at tin cans or other targets. However, before shooters can become proficient at plinking they must develop some shooting skills. There is no better way to hone one's shooting skills than by shooting at a target. Actually, most slingshot shooters will spend more time shooting at targets than at anything else. Since target practice is so important, it is prudent to spend some time, and effort, devising a high-quality target system.

SAFETY CONSIDERATIONS

When setting up a shooting range, safety is a primary consideration. Be sure no one can walk in the line-of-fire (rope it off) and be sure there will be no ricochet shots (large backstop). If slingshot shooting is to proliferate, as a sport, it is imperative that it has a good safety reputation.

Avoid ricochets -- For safety reasons, the target system must be set up to avoid damage or injury due to ricocheted projectiles. Every effort must be taken to protect the shooter, other people, and property in the area. This means the target area must be free of hard surfaces such as metal. Wood will slow down a projectile but a ricochet off a wood surface may still contain enough energy to do damage (especially if it strikes a person in the eye).

Errant shots -- No matter how good a shooter becomes, there is always the possibility that a shot may go in some unexpected direction. For this reason, the target setup should allow for errant shots that may cause damage.

PRACTICAL SYSTEMS

Bull's-eye -- The standard slingshot competition target has a 10-centimeter bull's-eye (3.9 inches), which is shot at from a distance of 10 meters. Any sheet of paper with a 10-centimeter bull's-eye will suffice as a target, but thick paper (or cardboard) works best. On special occasions I use targets made of one-inch thick Styrofoam—the BBs make a nice neat round hole in the Styrofoam.

Even though the standard shooting distance is 10 meters, when competing at a tournament, there is generally auxiliary competition that requires shooting at greater distances. Therefore, it is prudent to occasionally practice at 20-, 30-, and 40-meters.

Projectile retrieval -- If ammunition is not reused, practicing can become expensive. If practicing becomes expensive we don't practice as much as we should—we don't want that. Therefore, a target system should provide some means of retrieving the BBs for reuse.

A carpet (nylon netting or canvas) can be used as a backstop for the BBs. If the carpet is hung from the top, and allowed to hang freely, it will "give" when the BB strikes which helps prevent penetration. Thick, closely woven carpets work best. Pieces of used carpets can often be gotten from a carpeting store, or installer, for free. The carpet backstop will stop glass BBs, steel BBs, or lead BBs with no damage or distortion to the BB. Another carpet, placed at the bottom of the target can be used to collect the BBs as they fall off the backstop. If steel BBs get scattered on the ground, a magnet on a stick (available at most hardware stores) can be used to help retrieve them.

Figure 5-1 shows my personal 10-meter target system. The stovepipe at the top covers a roll (three feet wide) of butcher's wrapping paper. Several circles, representing bull's-eyes, are drawn on the wrapping paper. When the circles become riddled with holes, I simply cut off the paper, roll down fresh paper, and draw new circles. (The chain, seen in the photo, helps keep the paper from blowing around on windy days.)

Figure 5-1. My personal 10-meter target system in my back yard.

Indoor shooting range -- One of the great things about slingshot shooting is that you can generally set up an indoor shooting range. The indoor range can be used in winter, when it is too cold for outdoor shooting, or when the weather outside is prohibitive. Basements or garages are excellent places to set up a shooting range, but an attic should also be considered.

You may not have adequate space indoors for a standard 10-meter shooting range but that is not a critical problem. If the range is set up at a shorter distance, make the bull's-eye a little smaller than standard. Hitting the smaller bull's-eye will require just as much accuracy as the larger one at a greater distance. (There are trajectory complications when shooting at the shorter distance but they are small compared to the greater good of regular practice time.) The technical part of shooting (stance, anchor point, release, etc) will all require the same precision as a target set at 10 meters.

When designing an indoor target range, arrange the lighting so that you can see the BB's trajectory (illuminate the back side of BB). This provides subliminal feedback to the part of your brain that does the aiming.

ALTERNATIVE RANGES

If you are unable to set up a private shooting range, do the next best thing. Find our where the BB-gun shooters go for practice. If you join their organization, they may let you practice with your slingshot. Also, check out the archery and pistol ranges. If these ranges are not set up for slingshot shooting, encourage them to do so. Their business may benefit if they can accommodate slingshot shooters.

ALTERNATIVE TARGETS

Paint balls -- When you are just out plinking, sometimes it isn't easy to find a good target. Here's what I do in those cases: I shoot at something, like a tree stump, using a paint ball for ammunition. Then, I use the paint spot as a target for shooting steel BBs.

On some surfaces the steel BB leaves a strike mark on the paint, making it easy to see the impact point.

Plasterboard -- Pieces of discarded plasterboard make good targets. The BB imbeds into the board but generally does not penetrate all the way through. A plasterboard target, with shiny BBs imbedded in it, makes for a good keepsake (if it demonstrates a good shot pattern).

Sand target -- A sand pile makes a good target for several reasons; it is easy to see where the BBs strike (by the impact eruption), it heals itself for the next shot, and it does not damage the BB. If you can't find a suitable pile of sand, to use as a target, you can make your own. Build a sand box with sides about 5-inches deep. Fill the box to a depth of about 2-inches with sand (dirt or sawdust also works relatively well). Then, tilt up one side of the box until the sand almost starts to move to the low side—you have a sand target. (The slope of the sand box depends on the *angle-of-repose* for the particular type of sand you use.) Over time the sand will migrate to the low side of the box, use a shovel to move it back up to the top. By shoveling the sand through a screen the BBs can be retrieved.

Moving targets -- Sooner or later you may have the urge to shoot at a moving target. Targets can be rolled across your field of vision, thrown up, or made to swing back and forth. When you first start, shooting at a moving target can be a daunting experience. But, like shooting at a stationary target, you will become more accurate with practice.

When first starting, use a large target. As you become more accurate, target size can be reduced. If the target is rotating (rolling) when you shoot, it is difficult to determine where you hit relative to center by examining the holes. Examining the impact point does not indicate whether you hit high, low, left, or right of center. For that reason you must use a projectile whose trajectory is easily seen. This can be done by using white (glass or plastic) BBs and/or adjust the lighting so that the backside of the BB is illuminated.

Shooting at sporting clays can be an exciting challenge. Have someone stand behind a barrier and throw the clay up 10 to 15 feet into the air. (Be sure the person throwing the clays is protected from flying pieces of clays.) For best results, shoot when the clay is at the top of its flight because it is moving slowest at that point. Be cautioned: When you shoot up into the air the projectile will carry a long distance. Be sure there is no person or sensitive property within range of the projectile.

If you have a group (or family) of shooters, try shooting at soap bubbles. Kids love to make the bubbles and the adults love to shoot at them. Use the large (2- to 5-inch) bubble makers.

Other potential moving targets may include paper airplanes, Frisbees, rubber balls, paper plates, and cardboard disks. With a little thought I'm sure you can add to this list.

SLINGSHOT SHOOTING

CHAPTER 6

HANDEDNESS

DEFINITION

Shooters that pull the pouch back with their right hand, while holding the sling with their left hand, are said to be shooting with a **right-handed** stance. That is; the hand that is used to pull the pouch back defines handedness. (Similarly, with archers, the hand that pulls the bowstring back defines the handedness.)

Do right-handed people always shoot with a right-handed stance? Usually, but not always. There are several factors (many conflicting) that must be considered before choosing the best stance for an individual.

DOMINANT EYE

The *dominant eye* is the eye that is in charge of reporting vision to the brain. (The dominant eye looks directly at an object; the non-dominant eye looks at an object from the side.) Even though most people have a dominant eye, it is of little consequence in normal everyday living. However, dominant eye **is** an important consideration when we aim. When given a choice, we all prefer to aim with our dominant eye.

> Note: To find your dominant eye, point your finger at a distant object. Alternately close one eye then the other, whichever eye maintains the alignment of your finger and the object, is your dominant eye.

Most people, that have a dominant eye, have the same handedness. That is, right-handed people are generally right-eye dominant and left-handed people are generally left-eye dominant. This makes it easy for shooters to hold the pouch with their dominant hand near their dominant eye and use the bands and sling as a reference when aiming.

Aiming becomes a problem when the pouch hand and the dominant eye are opposite. In these cases, the line-of-aim is several inches from the projectile's path, which results in a condition called **convergence**. This means that the projectile's path crosses the line-of-sight at only one specific distance. The sight, of the slingshot, can be set for that specific distance (where projectile's path and sight cross) but it will be inaccurate at any other distance. It should be noted that dominant eye is not a principal factor when the instinctive aiming technique is used.

STEADIEST HAND

The sling hand makes all the adjustments when aiming while the pouch hand remains anchored to a specific point (anchor point). For example, if the initial alignment of the sling is to the left of the target the sling hand must move the sling to the right.

Therefore, it stands to reason that the steadiest hand should be used to hold the sling. Right-handed people are almost always steadiest with their right hand. This is a dilemma because using this reasoning; right-handed shooters should hold the *sling,* not the pouch, with their right hand.

PULLING STRENGTH

Another consideration in selecting a right- or left-handed stance is the strength of the pouch-pulling hand. The strongest hand (and arm) should logically be used for pulling the pouch back, which would be the right hand for a right-handed shooter. Not a lot of pulling power is required to pull the pouch back on a slingshot (usually between 10 and 20 pounds). However, this may become an issue if you're in a contest that requires shooting fast and frequently. In these cases, fatigue in the pulling hand and arm may be a consideration.

LOADING AND HOLDING POUCH

Right-handed shooters usually prefer to load the pouch with their right hand (better hand and finger dexterity). And, it is easier to hold the pouch in full draw position because the right-hand arm and fingers are stronger. Therefore, both dexterity and strength favor the right-handed person to shoot with a right-handed stance.

SELECTING THE BEST STANCE

As indicated, there are advantages and disadvantages of shooting either right- or left-handed regardless of the shooters normal handedness. Generally, the biggest consideration in selecting a right- or left-handed stance is dominant eye. Most shooters that are right handed, and right-eye dominant, shoot right handed, and vice versa for left-handed shooters. If shooters are right eye/hand dominant, but have trouble holding the sling steady with their left hand, (like me) they should try shooting with a left-handed stance. (I am right handed and right-eye dominant but shoot with a left-handed stance.)

A person that is just starting to shoot slingshots should try shooting both with a left and right-handed stance. Shoot a few hundred shots each way and see which is more accurate. Notice! I did not say, "Which stance *feels best*". Accuracy is much more important than feelings; no matter which stance you choose, it will "*feel best*" after a few thousand shots.

CHAPTER 7

SHOOTING TECHNIQUE

BODY POSITION

All shooters possess different levels of muscle coordination, strength, and dexterity. And, everyone is built a little differently, so individual shooting styles will vary among shooters because of physical ability and stature. You are encouraged to experiment, during practice, with different body positions and shooting styles until you find what is best suited to you as an individual. Once you have determined your best body position and shooting style it must be practiced and refined. **Do not** deviate from your style during competition—**consistency** is paramount for shooting accuracy.

When you are first learning to shoot a slingshot, try for consistency of form not target accuracy. Grade your practice session on how well you maintained your body position. Don't be afraid to experiment with new systems and techniques. But be aware, you may not shoot well when you first start using a new system; even if it is a good change, sometimes it takes a while for the benefits to emerge.

Foot position -- The ideal foot position is one that makes the upper body stable while executing a shot.

If you're stable, even a gust of wind, from any direction, will not move your aim off target. **Figure 7-1** shows two common stances. They are called the *square stance* and the *open stance*. In the "square" stance the tips of the toes are aligned with the target. In the "open" stance the front foot is turned outward about 45 degrees and is from 2 to 6 inches inside the line of aim. The ball, or toes, of the rear foot is placed on the aim line. The open stance is commonly accepted as being the best foot position. It is generally recommended that the distance between the heals should be the width of the shoulders. (I personally prefer a slightly wider stance.)

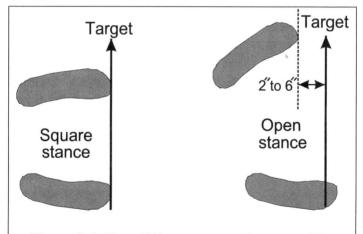

Figure 7-1. Two different types of stances. The open stance is generally accepted as being the better of the two.

In competition, when you find the perfect foot positions, do **not** move your feet between shots.

Shoulders -- The shoulders should be at the same angle, to the line-of-aim, as the feet. That is, if the square foot stance is used then the shoulders should be parallel to the line of aim. If the open foot stance is used the front shoulder should be slightly farther from the aim line than the rear shoulder. Don't be too concerned about the shoulders; they will generally assume the correct position if the other body parts are in the proper position.

Arms -- The forearm of the pouch arm should be in line with the draw force **(figure 7-2)**. It should be horizontal (or nearly so) when the bands are at full draw. The most common stance error is where the pouch-arm elbow is held too low. Holding the elbow a little high is acceptable form; however, holding the elbow a little too low is unacceptable.

Figure 7-2. The forearm, of the pulling arm, should be kept in line with the bands.

The sling arm must be held straight toward the target with the elbow either locked in position or with a slight bend. A locked elbow is best for consistency but some shooters prefer a slight bend at the elbow because it acts as a shock absorber when the pouch is released. Shooters with relatively short arms are more inclined to lock their elbow in order to attain maximum draw length.

Arm positions are a critical part of accuracy. Therefore, particular attention should be paid to arm positions on every shot. Be particularly conscious of arm positions when you first start a practice session.

Body -- The trunk of the body should be vertical when shooting. Some shooters have a tendency to bend forward at the hips or lean toward the target. The problem is that the "bent position" is difficult to duplicate consistently, especially during long practice sessions or tournaments. After several hours of practice, the body may start to bend, more or less, than when first starting the practice session.

Head -- The proper turn of the head is generally not a problem if the other body parts are in the proper position. Some shooters have a tendency to "tilt" the head toward the pouch side (eyes not level). Perception becomes distorted when the head is cocked to the side. We spend our entire lives looking at things, judging distances and angles, with our eyes level. Since we have practiced this way every waking hour of our lives, it seems reasonable that we should use the same viewing technique when aiming and shooting a slingshot. When shooting a slingshot, the head should be held such that the **eyes are level**!

THE MECHANICS OF SHOOTING

Draw length -- The length of your sling arm, and location of your anchor point, dictate the length of your draw. The length of the draw affects the force required to attain full draw. The longer the draw (for any particular band) the more force that is required to bring the pouch back to full draw. (On some slingshots the draw length can be adjusted two or three inches.) If the force required to attain full draw is too great, or too little, the bands must be replaced. Replacement bands that are shorter or thicker will increase the required draw force. Bands that are longer or narrower require less pulling force. Keep in mind that the more force required to attain full draw, the more difficult it is to hold the slingshot steady.

Band twist -- In order to shoot accurately, the bands must not have any extraneous twist between the pouch and sling. Band twisting is a greater problem with flat bands than with tubular type bands. Generally, the shorter the bands and/or the stiffer the bands, the less tendency they have to twist. When using flat bands, a twist in the bands is obvious, when using tube-type bands a twist is not so noticeable (**figure 7-3**). An index line can be scribed on the tubular band to make any twist more obvious.

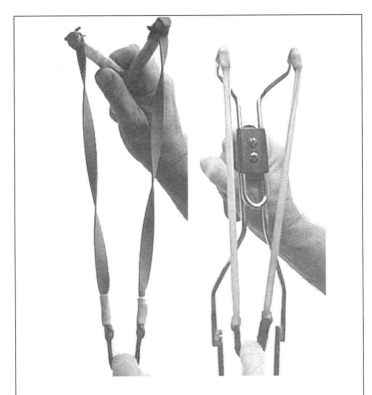

Figure 7-3. The twist in the flat bands, on the left, is obvious; the twist in the tubular bands, on the right, is not so obvious.

After each shot, the bands must be checked for twist. To remove the twist, the pouch must be rotated. This is best done immediately after the shot and before reaching for another BB.

Cant angle -- The "*cant angle*" is the angle, from vertical, that the slingshot is held when shooting (**figure 7-4**). Most shooters find it more comfortable to hold the sling handle at some angle (cant angle) other than straight up (vertical). The exact angle is not extremely important but **consistency** is. The cant angle for different shooters range from zero (vertical) to nearly 90 degrees (horizontal). Most shooters hold the sling between 30-and 50-degrees from vertical. There are three important considerations when deciding what cant angle is best for you. First, is it easy for you to orient the pouch at that same angle? Second, does the cant angle allow a good reference point (sight) on or near the sling for aiming? (When using the instinctive aiming technique you don't have to be concerned with this reference point.) If one of the forks obscures the bull's-eye, the orientation of the sling, or the anchor point, must be changed. And third, is it repeatable with precision?

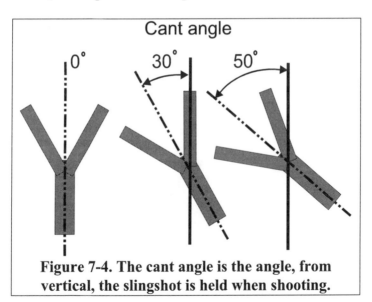

Figure 7-4. The cant angle is the angle, from vertical, the slingshot is held when shooting.

Once you determine the cant angle best suited to you, you must use this exact same orientation for every shot. In order to do this, it is best to use some sort of vertical reference. (It's much easier to judge when a reference is perfectly vertical than to judge an off-vertical angle.) One of the forks can be used as a vertical reference (the 30 degree cant angle shown in **figure 7-4** is an example) or some other reference can be attached to the sling. **Figure 7-5** shows a vertical reference attached to the yoke of a sling. When shooting, it is a simple matter to hold the reference vertical thus insuring that the sling is at the proper cant angle.

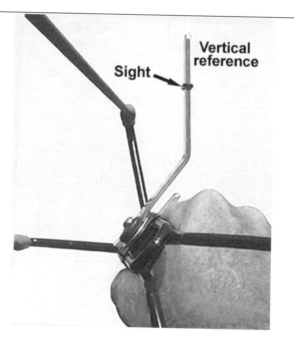

Figure 7-5. The vertical reference, on this slingshot, is used to help insure proper cant angle. (On this slingshot it is also used to attach a sight.)

A bubble-level can be used to insure proper cant angle. The bubble-level can be attached to the sling as shown in **figure 7-6**. Permanently attach the bubble level to the sling such that the bubble is centered when holding the sling at the desired cant angle. Bubble-levels can be purchased from most hardware stores for a few dollars and attached to the sling with superglue.

Figure 7-6. When the bubble in the level is centered, the sling is at the proper cant angle.

I personally use a cant angle of 50 degrees. I maintain consistency by using a vertical sight as shown in **figure 7-5**.

Sling rotation -- If one of the forks is rotated farther forward than the other (**rotation** or **twist**), the projectile will be thrown off-course because one band will pull harder, and faster, than the other. If a tendency for improper sling rotation is not detected early on (when a person is first learning to shoot), it may remain for that person's entire shooting career. **Figure 7-7** shows an improper sling rotation. Improper rotation is usually a problem only when the supporting fingers are used to hold the forks as shown in **figure 7-7**. When a wrist brace is used, the problem is not so prevalent.

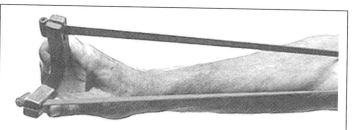

Figure 7-7. Improper sling rotation. In this example, the bottom fork is farther forward than the top fork. Consequently, the bottom band is stretched farther than the top band.

It is difficult to check your own stance for proper sling rotation. Therefore, it is advisable to have someone else check for improper rotation while you hold the pouch at full draw in shooting position. Once the proper rotation is achieved the shooter must memorize that position and repeat it for all succeeding shots.

There is another way to check for improper rotation: Hold the sling in shooting position and pull back the pouch until the bands become taut. If one band becomes taut before the other, there is a rotation problem.

Wrist support -- If your slingshot has a wrist support, be sure to use it properly. The wrist support helps keep the yoke in proper position without overstressing the wrist. Without the wrist support, the forks of the yoke have a tendency to tilt backwards as the pouch is being pulled. When the pouch is released the yoke snaps forward and downward. This uncontrolled movement of the yoke causes accuracy errors.

When pulling the bands back, the wrist muscles must allow the support to press snugly against the forearm. Hold the handle only tight enough to maintain control. To maximize accuracy, the pressure of the support, on the forearm, must be the same for every shot.

Loading the pouch -- Before loading the pouch, make sure the bands are not twisted. This will insure that you load the proper side of the pouch. It is advisable to mark the pouch with colored indelible ink so the proper side can easily be identified.

When loading, make sure the BB is in the center of the pouch. If the BB is not centered, it will be like altering your anchor point and the shot will miss its intended target. After loading, and before grasping the pouch, make sure the ends of the pouch are aligned (see **figure 7-8**). Always grasp the pouch the same way for every shot, in particular, be sure the thumb is always holding the center of the pouch directly over the BB.

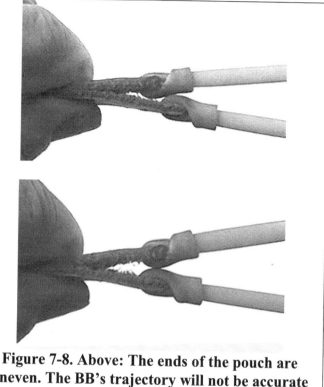

Figure 7-8. Above: The ends of the pouch are uneven. The BB's trajectory will not be accurate because the top band is pulling harder than the bottom band. Below: The proper pouch alignment, both ends of the pouch are even.

Once you have loaded the pouch, and have gotten into your shooting stance, stand quietly for a moment (pause) and look at the target—visualize the BB striking the center of the bull's-eye. The pause and visualization helps key the "right-brain" as to the desired outcome.

Pulling the pouch -- The draw technique can be different for each individual. The draw can start with the sling above the aim line and the pouch drawn back as the sling is lowered into shooting position. Or, the pouch can be pulled while bringing the sling up from below. Some shooters prefer to position the sling at arms length, on the aim line, before pulling the pouch back. These differences don't serve any functional purpose and can be simply attributed to the shooters *style*.

Note: If a band is going to break, it usually happens *while* the pouch is being drawn back. Therefore, if the bands are brought to full draw, before the pouch is positioned on the face, getting hit in the face with the broken band will be avoided. Obviously, shooting style can *save face*.

Pouch anchor point -- When executing a shot, the pouch is drawn back to some point then held for a moment before releasing. The point at which it is held is called the *"anchor point"*. The more consistent the anchor point, the better the accuracy. (An error of $1/4$ inch in the anchor-point position will cause an error of nearly 4 inches at a target 10-meters away.) Some shooters draw the pouch all the way back behind their ear when shooting. This technique provides a long draw but is not conducive to consistency. A better technique is to establish an anchor point somewhere on the face.

An anchor point must be chosen that is functional, comfortable, and, most importantly, repeatable. For best aim, the anchor point should be at, or very near, the aiming eye. The problem with holding the pouch at the eye is that when the pouch is released the pouch hand moves back slightly and may touch the eye area, which will cause a flinch at a critical time. Even if the hand doesn't actually hit the eye, the anticipation of being hit may cause a flinch. If an anchor point is chosen that is too far from the eye, there will be a problem with convergence (the shot will only be accurate where the aim and the path of the BB converge).

Most archers use the corner of their mouth as an anchor point. This technique is acceptable for the slingshot shooter as well. To aid in establishing the corner of the mouth, as the anchor point, bite on a wooden pencil with the eraser end protruding slightly from the edge of the mouth. The thumb of the pouch hand can be brought back to the eraser for an exceptionally stable and repeatable anchor point.

> The nail of the thumb can be rested on the eraser, for relief, for a short time, before releasing the pouch. The resting position is especially valuable when hunting. The pouch, occasionally, must be held at full draw while waiting for the critter to present a suitable target.

An anchor point directly on the cheekbone may be a good compromise between the eye and the mouth because it is not far from the line of sight, is unlikely to cause a flinch, and is easy to duplicate with every shot (consistency).

> I used my cheekbone as an anchor point for many years. The last time I was slapped in the face, by a broken band, I decided to change the anchor point to the corner of my mouth. My accuracy suffered for a short period, but now I am happy with the change.

Some safety glasses are designed such that they interfere with the anchor point. If the thumb touches any part of the glasses, there is a proclivity to flinch because the eye is sensitive to the movement of the glasses. If this occurs, replace the glasses with a pair that doesn't interfere with the anchor point. Remember, the equipment must conform to your shooting style—not vise versa.

> Because the pouch hand jerks back upon releasing the pouch, an anchor point anywhere on the face may cause some shooters to flinch. With a great deal of concentrated effort, any shooter can eliminate the flinch problem. Some potentially great shooters may not even be aware that they have a flinch problem and consequently may never reach their accuracy potential.

Pouch orientation -- The axis of the pouch must be orientated at the same angle as the cant angle of the sling. That is, if the sling handle is held vertically the pouch must also be held vertically. If the sling handle is held at a cant angle of 30 degrees to the right, the axes of the pouch must also be held 30 degrees to the right. If the pouch orientation is not the same as the cant angle, the pouch will twist as it is released. The twist will cause the projectile to be thrown off course.

The best way to check your pouch angle is with the use of a mirror. Stand in front of a mirror and bring the pouch back to full draw, then, orient the pouch to the cant angle. Memorize the feeling of the proper pouch orientation. Periodically test yourself, in front of a mirror, to make sure the pouch angle has remained consistent with the cant angle.

Proper orientation of the pouch can be difficult if a radical cant angle is employed. If this is the case, both the cant angle and pouch orientation must be changed. When deciding on the angle, from vertical, that you hold the sling, be sure you are able to hold the pouch at that same angle.

Even the experienced shooter will sometimes forget to properly orient the pouch before release. For that reason, the orientation should be done as a distinct operation in itself. The pouch should be held vertically as the bands are drawn back; when full draw is reached, the pouch must then be oriented (see **figure 7-9**). When pouch orientation is incorporated into the shot routine, as a separate and distinct operation, it is unlikely to be overlooked.

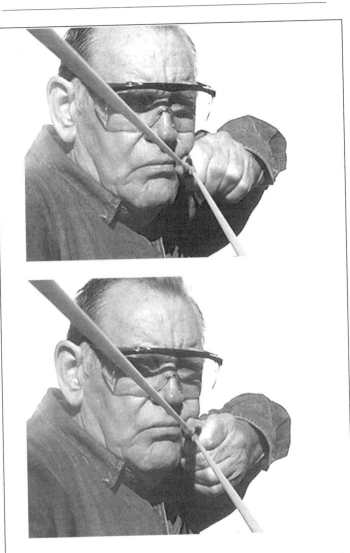

Figure 7-9. As shown in the top photo, the apex of the pouch is held vertically as it is brought back to full draw. Then, the wrist is turned so that the pouch is oriented to the cant angle of the sling as shown in the lower photo.

Pouch release -- When shooting with a gun, it is advisable to *slowly* squeeze the trigger. Jerking or pulling the trigger quickly will cause the gun to move and the target missed. Therefore, slowly releasing the pouch, when shooting a slingshot, would seem to be a reasonable correlation. Actually, it is not. When pulling a trigger, the muscles in the hand must be <u>contracted</u> which causes the jerk. But with the slingshot, the pouch release requires the <u>relaxation</u> (not contraction) of the muscles. The relaxing of a muscle generally does not cause a jerk even if it is done quickly.

Unfortunately there is an inherent problem with pouch release that causes errors. The pouch is held between the thumb and the side of the bent index finger. Friction between the fingers and pouch keep it from releasing before intended. As the pressure on the pouch is lessened, it slips from between the fingers and is propelled away by the tension in the bands. The problem is that when the pouch is allowed to slowly slip away it may slip from one finger slightly before the other. This means one side of the pouch will proceed ahead of the other (accuracy error). To minimize this problem, it is suggested that you consciously try to release the pouch as quickly as possible without jerking.

When one side of the pouch advances ahead of the other, or one side of the pouch gets blown (from aerodynamic wind pressure) into or around the BB, the BB will go astray. The BB may strike the fork, the hand, or the band causing damage or injury.

When the pouch is released, the projectile is only just starting to accelerate toward the target. The *lock time* is slower for slingshots than firearms and air guns. (Lock time is the time between the release of the pouch and the time the BB leaves the pouch.) Therefore, you must maintain your *sight picture*, for a short time, after the pouch is released, in order to obtain maximum accuracy.

BREATH CONTROL

Normal breathing is accompanied by a rhythmic movement of the chest, stomach, and shoulder area. These factors make it impossible to hold a slingshot perfectly steady while breathing. The breath cycle includes the process of inhaling, exhaling, and then a short pause (respiratory pause) before the cycle is repeated. The natural respiratory pause may last 2 or 3 seconds. However, the respiratory pause can be extended for 10 to 15 seconds, without discomfort, by deliberately taking deeper breaths. Aiming and shooting should be done during the respiratory pause. If the shot is not taken during the pause, the breathing cycle should be repeated from the beginning.

> The forgoing is the accepted standard breath control technique for all types of shooting. However, for some people it doesn't work very well. I personally feel uncomfortable letting my breath out before aiming and shooting. I like to aim and shoot while holding a deep breath. Try it both ways to determine which way is more comfortable for you.

Breathing should be integrated with the rest of the mechanics of the shot routine. That is, when you are loading the pouch you should be taking deep breaths—a deep breath cycle should be taken while you pause and look at the target—inhale deeply as you bring the slingshot up and draw the pouch back—breath out then pause while aiming and releasing.

INTEGRATING SHOT PROCESSES

To execute a shot, all of the shot processes must be integrated into a single routine for each shot. The following checklist should be used to combine all of the shot processes.

Stance
> Look at the target
> Move front foot into position
> Move back foot into position
> Look at target again
> If needed, readjust both foot positions
> Check distance between heals

Load pouch
> Center the BB in pouch
> Align front edges of pouch
> Position pouch between thumb and forefinger
> Check for centering of BB in fingers

Stand straight

Look at target
> Pause and breath deeply
> Visualize hitting the bull's-eye

Bring sling up and draw bands

Establish proper cant angle
Check sling rotation
Establish anchor point
Orient pouch to cant angle
Check:
    Drawing elbow
    Sling elbow
Control breathing
Aim
Maximize concentration
Release pouch
Pause in shooting position

Memorize this checklist. It shouldn't be hard because it only describes what you do (or should be doing) every time you shoot a shot. With practice, these steps will become automatic.

SLINGSHOT SHOOTING

CHAPTER 8

AIMING

There are two types of aiming techniques used by slingshot shooters—the *instinctive technique* and the *sight technique*, both types will be examined.

INSTINCTIVE SHOOTING

Instinctive shooting (or instinctive aiming) is a way of shooting without consciously aiming (with sights). Both eyes are focused on the target; the orientation of the sling and bands are registered with the peripheral vision. With this technique the shooter "*feels*" the aim rather than sees it. When the alignment of the sling and bands "*feels right*" the pouch is released. One advantages of instinctive shooting is that it automatically compensates for distance. That makes the instinctive shooting technique excellent for plinking and hunting where the distance to the target is not the same for every shot. For target shooting, where shooting distance is more or less uniform, aiming with a sight is more accurate. An advantage of using the instinctive shooting technique is that it doesn't matter which eye is dominant and therefore you can shoot with either hand.

SLINGSHOT SHOOTING

> One problem with instinctive shooting is that it must be relearned (to some extent) every time a new slingshot, with different drawing force and BB speed, is used (trajectory is different).

The secret of instinctive shooting is being able to visualize the trajectory of the projectile while aligning the slingshot. In order to visualize the trajectory, the mind must build up a memory bank of every conceivable type of shot. All of the different types of shots like long shots, short shots, and inclined shots must be executed and recorded in the mind's memory bank. All of this memorizing can be done while plinking and hunting, or, with formal practice using targets. Here are some things to remember if a formal practice routine is used:

1. For efficient learning, both the trajectory of the BB and the point of impact must be seen and recorded in the mind's memory bank. If the shooter can't see the BB it may mean that he is flinching (blinking) on releasing the pouch.
2. Flinching during the shot will prevent seeing the trajectory and point of impact. This hinders the learning process.
3. Learning is much more efficient when there is **immediate** feedback. For example, it is much better to be able to see where the BB strikes (when shot) than to have to go look at the target to find out where the BB struck.
4. Shooting with the sun at your back will help you see the path of the projectile better. Lights in an

indoor target range should be positioned such that they illuminate the backside of the projectile.

5. The smaller the projectile, the harder it is to see. This is not only because it is small but also because it generally travels faster. This is a good reason to practice with BBs that are at least $^3/_8$-inch in diameter.

6. When shooting, be sure to keep both eyes open.

AIMING WITH A SIGHT

Aiming, with the use of a sight, is much more accurate (for target shooting) than the instinctive shooting technique. By sight, I mean any reference point on the sling, or sling hand, that is used for the purpose of aligning the eye, and sling, with the target. If a suitable reference point is not available, on the slingshot, an actual sight can be attached to the sling. The process of aiming requires the eye, slingshot sight, and bull's-eye to be in perfect alignment.

The dominant eye is generally used for aiming. The other eye can either be kept open or closed; whatever you decide, do it consistently. For most shooters the pouch, at full draw, will be on the same side of the face as the dominant eye. That is, if you are right-eye dominant, the pouch will be drawn back with the right hand, to the right side of the face. If you are right-eye dominant and use the left hand to draw the pouch to the left side of the face, **convergence** will be a problem if the distance to the target is not constant.

Convergence is where the line-of-aim is some distance away from the path of the projectile. When the slingshot sight is set for a specific distance the line-of-aim and path of the projectile meet (or converge) at the target. At any other distance, the sight will be inaccurate. The farther the line-of-aim is, from the path of the projectile, the greater the problem with convergence.

Using a sight is advantageous when shooting with several different slingshots each having a different configuration and draw force. Once the sight is set for a specific slingshot, with specific bands, it will shoot accurately without consciously having to adjust aim for draw force. Transitioning from a target slingshot with weak bands to a hunting slingshot with strong bands is not a problem when a sight is used.

Move-through technique -- It is difficult to hold the sight on the exact center of a target without moving somewhat. The *move-through* aiming technique does not require that the aim be held steady on target. Instead, the aim is moved in a horizontal figure-eight pattern with the bull's-eye at the point where the lines intersect. The move-through aiming method requires that the pouch be released as the aim is anticipated to move over the bull's-eye. Obviously, the timing of the release is of vital importance when using this aiming method. With practice the timing will get better and so will accuracy.

The line-of-aim does not necessarily have to be moved in a figure-eight pattern. Back-and-forth or up-and-down patterns are also a commonly used.

Probably the most common move-through technique (and has the least structure) starts from wherever the aim is first established then moved toward the bull's eye; the pouch is released when the aim moves over the bull's eye.

> To become proficient with this aiming technique the speed at which the aim is moved must be uniform and constant from shot to shot. Generally, the slower the aim is moved, the more accurate the shot will be.

Hold-steady technique -- When using the *hold-steady* aiming technique the objective is to position the sight on the bull's-eye, hold steady on target, and then release the pouch. With practice, this technique is a little more accurate than the move-through technique. In practicing this technique, occasionally try to hold the aim on the bull's-eye for as long as possible before releasing. However, when shooting for maximum accuracy, the holding time should be brief. After a short period of time the eye loses its acuity, the muscles begin to fatigue, and mental anxiety begins; therefore, the aiming process should not be longer than 4 to 6 seconds.

> The stronger the bands, the harder it is to hold steady on target. This is a good reason to use relatively weak bands for target shooting.

AIMING AND TIMING

When shooting a shot, most of the physical and mental procedures are done with a specific timing. That is, the pouch is loaded at a specific pace, the pause before pulling the bands is a specific length of time, pulling the bands is done at a specific pace, and so on. Each of these activities is done with a specific timing, or rhythm, that develops over a long period of time. The timing is subconscious and therefore is done automatically without conscious thought. This is all well and good and generally promotes accuracy. HOWEVER! This subconscious rhythm can cause a big problem.

The subconscious mind wants to carry things too far; it wants to incorporate the actual aiming process into a rhythm as well. This is detrimental to accuracy because the aiming process has random aspects. The target is not always acquired in a specific length of time. But, the subconscious mind wants to shoot in a certain period of time regardless of whether the target is acquired or not. This tendency must be fought at all cost.

Do not let rhythm sneak into your aiming process! Do not release the pouch until the target is acquired regardless of how long it takes. It is tempting to settle for less than accurate sighting at the time of release. Resign yourself to be a perfectionist when aiming and releasing. If you accept less than perfection you will never force yourself to perform at your highest potential.

WINDAGE ADJUSTMENTS

The shorter the distance to a target, the less one has to be concerned about windage. At a target distance of 10 meters, no windage correction is necessary for winds up to about five mph. However, when shooting at a target beyond 10 meters, or under high wind conditions, aim has to be adjusted to account for windage. There are three major parameters that must be considered when shooting in windy conditions. They are; projectile speed, wind speed, and wind direction.

Every type of projectile will be affected, to some extent, by wind. The size, weight, and density of the projectile must be considered when determining a correction for windage.

Projectile speed -- The wind only affects the flight of the projectile while it is on its way to the target. The longer it takes to reach the target the more it will be affected. For example, a projectile traveling at 100 feet/sec will require about twice the correction as one traveling at 200 feet/sec. Therefore, the faster the projectile, the less aim has to be adjusted for any given wind condition. This is good reason to use the strongest (fastest) bands you can handle comfortably.

Wind speed -- The speed of the wind obviously affects the trajectory of the projectile. Twice the wind speed will have about twice the effect on the projectile.

Judging wind speed can be a problem. Our senses aren't very good at judging wind speed; after a 20 mph gust, a 10 mph wind may seem like a 5 mph wind. Flags, ribbons, or dropping dirt or grass can be used to help judge wind speed. However, if you are serious about accuracy, the best solution is to use a commercial wind gage (anemometer). Using an instrument has the advantage of representing wind speed as a number. Having a number to work with is much better than having to use subjective terms like fast or slow. Hand-held wind speed indicators, used by archers and hang gliding enthusiasts, are small, light, inexpensive and accurate.

If you don't want to buy a wind speed indicator, you should consider building your own. **Figure 8-1** shows how a rudimentary wind-speed indicator can be constructed using a ping-pong ball, an eight-inch long thread, and a protractor.

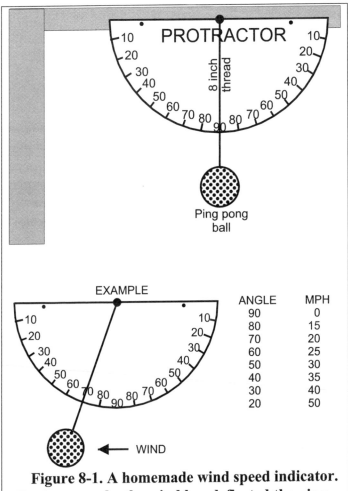

Figure 8-1. A homemade wind speed indicator. In the example, the wind has deflected the ping-pong ball to the 70-degree mark. The table indicates this would be a 20 mph wind.

Wind direction -- A wind that is perpendicular to the path of the projectile (cross wind) will have the greatest effect on the path of the projectile. Aim correction must be made toward the direction of the

103

wind. For example, if the wind is blowing from right to left, the aim correction must be to the right.

If the wind is parallel to the path of the projectile, it will either speed up or slow down the projectile (compared to a no wind condition) depending on whether the wind is blowing with or against the projectile. When shooting into the wind, the aim correction must be <u>up,</u> and with a tail wind, the aim correction must be <u>down</u>. These parallel windage corrections are small and can usually be ignored except when shooting long distances under extreme wind conditions.

When the wind is from some angle, other than parallel or perpendicular to the path of the projectile, the aim correction must be only a percentage of the perpendicular correction.

Calculating aim corrections -- The amount of correction for windage depends on several variables. These variables include distance to target, wind speed, wind direction, projectile weight, and projectile speed. All of these variables could be put into a mathematical equation and calculated with a computer in a microsecond. But if we wanted to do it that way we would be rocket scientist, not slingshot shooters. The slingshot shooter generally determines aim correction by experimentation.

When determining aim correction it is best to determine the correction required for a 10-meter shot with a cross wind of 10 mph. It is then an easy matter to multiply the correction, by some factor, if the wind condition, and distance, is greater than your reference parameters.

Pick a day when the wind is blowing at a steady speed. Set up your shot so that you are shooting at a distance of 10-meters perpendicular to the wind direction (cross wind). Using ³/₈-inch BBs, shoot about 10 shots aiming directly at the bull's-eye. Measure the horizontal distance the average shot missed the bull's-eye. Reverse the shooting direction and shoot 10 more shots. Average the error for both directions. With this data you can calculate how much a 10 mph wind will affect a 10-meter shot (to use as a standard).

Note: The preceding experimental data is accurate only when using a ³/₈-inch BB and one particular slingshot. Another slingshot that shoots at a different speed would have a different error. A BB that is different in size, or weight, would travel at a different speed, which would require a different correction.

Another aim correction technique -- There is another, much simpler, way to make the windage correction. Simply shoot a test shot, or series of shots, at the center of the bull's-eye and see how much the wind deflected the BB. On succeeding shots simply adjust aim to compensate for the error.

This windage correction technique works when practicing or plinking but generally won't work in tournament shooting. In tournaments you may not have the liberty of shooting a series of test shots. By the time you figure out wind correction you may have missed enough shots to cause you to lose the tournament.

CHAPTER 9

MIND AND BODY

ROUTINES

A routine is a systematically performed procedure, or activity, designed to standardize a specific task. Routines are imperative for consistent, accurate shooting. Physical routines insure that the shooters actions are the same for every shot. Mental routines are used to insure the mental processes are the same for each shot.

Physical routines -- A master instructor can advise you on how to hold and shoot a slingshot. When you shoot, the instructor can observe you to see if you followed instructions precisely. If you didn't, the instructor can tell you exactly what you did wrong. The physical routine, for each shot, is easy for you, and anyone else, to observe and therefore, any deviation from this routine is easy to detect. Having a good physical routine is essential to good shooting; any deviation from your normal routine can introduce errors.

An example of a typical physical routine is aligning the feet into shooting position. It could consist of: Look at target—move right foot into position—move left foot into position—check target position—readjust right foot—readjust left foot. If any of these things are omitted, or done out of turn,

107

the stance may not be correct. The routine is established so as to insure that the physical processes are done precisely and correctly each and every time.

Every aspect of shooting that **can** be conducted as a physical routine **should** be conducted as a physical routine. Your routine will allow you to perform at your maximum capability. You can, and should, experiment with techniques outside your normal routine. But, when maximum accuracy in mandatory, always trust your established routine to deliver the results.

Mental routines -- Mental routines work in conjunction with, and generally precede, the physical routine. A mental routine can be something as simple as talking to yourself. As an example, when preparing to execute a shot, the dialogue could go something like this: Check BB position in pouch—check breathing—check anchor point—concentrate on aim.

A mental routine doesn't necessarily have to be associated with a physical activity. It can stand alone as a strictly mental process. An example of this is the visualization of the trajectory of the BB before executing a shot.

Detecting errors in a mental routine is much more difficult than detecting errors in a physical routine. Observers (or coaches) can't see what is going on in your mind so they are not able to monitor and correct your mental routine. The only way you can detect flaws in your mental routine is to consciously and meticulously study it when you are shooting exceptionally well—then, when you aren't shooting well, check your mental routine for errors and omissions.

POSITIVE IMAGING

The concept of *positive thinking* has been around a long time. Positive thinking works reasonably well with abstract thoughts (thoughts that cannot be pictured) but it is not the best technique for substantive thoughts (thoughts that can be depicted by pictures). Thoughts such as "I <u>will</u> make this shot" or "I <u>will</u> put five shots in the bull's-eye," even if said repeatedly and with great conviction, will probably not help your shooting. Indeed, these thoughts usually do more harm than good because they can cause a *cycle-of-frustration* when a shot is missed or a tournament is lost.

Positive thinking is a "left-brain" activity. If the concept were changed to *positive imaging,* which is a "right-brain" activity, it would be a valuable tool in dealing with substantive issues like shooting a shot or winning a tournament. Positive imagery, or simply *imaging*, is the process of visualizing the desired action or result prior to execution. To use imaging you must imagine (picture) the BB hitting the center of the bull's-eye before the shot is executed. When shooting in a tournament you must also use imaging on a larger more encompassing scale. Imagine winning the entire tournament; imagine the congratulatory handshake, and imagine holding up the winner's trophy for all to see. Imagining all these things, as though they have already happened, programs the "right-brain" as to the desired result.

PHYSICAL CONDITIONING

Your ability to hold steady, at full draw, is directly related to the physical condition of the muscles used for slingshot shooting. Slingshot-shooting muscles are not used much in everyday activities. Shooting a slingshot takes a very few, but specific, muscles—it doesn't take much effort to build up these specific muscles. An exercise program, to develop shooting muscles, allows you to draw the pouch back easier, hold steady on target longer, and practice longer without fatigue. It is especially important to develop the shoulders and upper body. A good exercise program will help prevent *slingshot shoulder* (try saying that real fast).

To develop the sling arm and shoulder, hold a 5 to 10-pound weight at arms length. Move it in an 8-inch circle about 10 times. Then, repeat the exercise circling in the opposite direction. Rest for a while and then repeat the exercise using a horizontal figure-eight pattern instead of a circle. Repeat this entire exercise until you become fatigued. As you become stronger, increase the weight so the arm and shoulder muscles become increasingly stronger.

The pouch arm doesn't require much strength to pull the pouch to the anchor point, for this reason, it is often left out of the exercise routine. However, steadiness and fatigue resistance will improve as pulling strength increases. The best way to increase pulling strength is to simulate the pulling of the slingshot bands but with greater resistance. To do

110

this, attach an exercise spring to a wall or doorway. Brace the sling hand on the wall and pull the spring back with the arm and shoulder. Adjust the spring resistance and duration of exercise as you become increasingly stronger. As you progress, you can add to, or modify, this routine as you see fit for your personal physical fitness requirements.

A bow can be used as an exercise apparatus. (An out dated recurved bow can often be purchased at auction for a very reasonable price.) The draw action of the bow is usually stronger than a slingshot, therefore, repeatedly drawing the bow makes for a good exercise routine.

The benefits of physical exercise are not somewhere in the distant future; an increase in shooting consistency and accuracy will be observed almost immediately after initiating your exercise program. This is important because the quicker the improvement appears, the more inspirational the exercise will be, and thus, more likely to be made a regular routine.

SLINGSHOT SHOOTING

CHAPTER 10

PRACTICE

Despite the fact that the sport of slingshot shooting has been around for a long time, it has not yet reached its maturity. Therefore, there is no better time in history to become the best in the world at slingshot shooting. How good you can become is a combination of both natural talent *and* determination. In the future it will take both natural talent and dedication to practice to rise the top of the slingshot world. However, at the present time exceptional talent is not absolutely necessary to become the best. The only requirement is the desire to be great and the commitment to practice.

It is easy to be determined during a competitive game or tournament. But, in order to be great, you must have the same determination when practicing. How far up the ladder you progress will depend on the quality and quantity of your practice time.

PRACTICE TIME

How much practice time is required? The answer varies depending on the individual's ability, motivation, and expectations. Generally, the better you want to become the more time you must spend practicing. On average, Olympic champions in archery (a similar sport) practice five or six days a week shooting in excess of 150 arrows during each practice session. Victor Wunderle, an Olympics archery champion, reportedly trains ten hours per day, six days per week. His daily routine includes shooting for eight hours (about 450 arrows) then he spends two more hours on exercising and equipment repair. If you intend to become an Olympic champion, in slingshot shooting, (I expect slingshot shooting to be in the Olympics eventually) you will have to do likewise. Collegiate archers practice two or three times a week, each practice session is two or three hours long.

> Just imagine for a moment how good you could shoot if you were as dedicated to slingshot shooting as Victor Wunderle is to archery.

To become reasonably proficient at slingshot shooting, you should try to practice at least two or three times per week, and if possible, every day. If you only have a chance to practice once or twice a month it may take a long time before you achieve consistency and, thereby, accuracy. Probably the best way to gage the proper practice time is by the results you experience. If you win all the events you enter, you're probably practicing enough.

In general, the duration of your practice sessions should be no less than an hour and no less than 100 shots. However, the overriding factor, in governing the length of practice sessions, should be dictated by motivation. While you're motivated and shooting well, keep on practicing, but quit before you become bored and sloppy.

PRACTICE REGIMEN

We all have the capacity to do several things at one time but we can only focus on <u>one</u> thing at a time. This means we can't focus on aim, anchor point, etc. all at the same time. Therefore, we must train ourselves well enough so that some things are done automatically while we focus on something else. Each practice session should be broken down into segments; each segment should be a concentrated effort at perfecting a specific aspect of shooting so that it will become automatic. For example, take 10 shots while concentrating on anchor point, 10 shots while focusing on pouch release, then stance, aim, etc. After that, spend the rest of your practice session incorporating all the things you were concentrating on. If you are having difficulty with any particular aspect, concentrate your practice on that particular aspect. When you focus on an individual weak point, do not be too concerned about accuracy. But, before quitting your practice session, be sure to devote some time on accuracy.

There are some things that can be practiced without actually shooting. For example, you can practice loading the pouch while watching TV. It only takes a few weeks of casual practice to become proficient at loading without looking. You will appreciate this capability when you are squirrel hunting.

You can only be as accurate as you are steady. Hold a laser pointer at arms length and point at a spot on a wall. Practice pointing the laser at that spot while holding an exercise weight in the same hand.

Aiming, breathing, and anchor point consistency can also be practiced without actually shooting.

ACCURACY PLATEAU

Most shooters continue to improve until they reach a plateau where improvement slows or ceases. At this point you must initiate a critical analysis of every minute aspect of your shooting technique. Make a list of how you might improve each aspect. How could you make your anchor point more consistent? How could you make your aim steadier? Try to improve every little aspect of your shooting technique even if it is only a minute improvement. For example, if you normally control your anchor point to the nearest $\frac{1}{8}$ inch, you will have to cut the tolerance to $\frac{1}{16}$ inch. If you do this with every aspect of your stance and shooting technique, your accuracy will continue to improve.

EQUIPMENT AND ENVIRONMENT

When practicing, use the same equipment you use for competitive shooting. Don't save the new slingshot and don't put on new bands just before the big tournament. If tournament conditions require using several different slingshots and/or several different size BBs, be sure to practice with each. Practice under different weather, temperature, light, and wind conditions. In fact, you should deliberately seek out extreme environmental conditions just so you have experience with the extremes.

Make sure every article of clothing you wear in competition has been tested under practice conditions. Practice with loose clothes, tight clothes, heavy, and light clothes. You will learn which types of clothes affect your accuracy. Never compete, or even practice, with leather-soled shoes, they have a propensity for slipping.

RECORDS

All successful competitors thrive on the challenge. Each time you practice you should be challenged to do better. Bowlers have their game averages, golfers have their handicaps, and ball players have their batting averages. These numbers serve as a gauge as to how well a particular task is performed. Very often the numbers themselves represent the competition, which stimulates the challenge. Devise a system that numerically reflects your shooting accuracy. Then, record and chart the results of each practice session. Improving your record will serve as a challenge to your competitive nature and will stimulate improvement.

Setting numerical goals helps to encourage practice. When setting goals, be sure they are time dependent. For example, your goal may be to get fifty percent of your shots in the 10-centimeter bull's-eye in two months. This type of goal encourages a high frequency of practice in the next two months to insure the improvement. In contrast, if your goal is to improve X percent each time you practice, it doesn't contain a built-in incentive to practice frequently.

117

Once you start shooting good scores you may realize you can become a serious competitor. Then, you will be more inclined to invest more time and effort to improving your skills. The more time and effort you invest, the better you will become; the better you become, the more time and effort you will invest (sounds like an inspirational cycle).

VIDEO REVIEW

Videotaping, and reviewing, your practice sessions can be a very revealing exercise. When you view the tape, critique yourself. Here are some video-viewing pointers:

1. Observe your form when you are shooting well; compare this to when you are in a shooting slump.
2. Is your anchor point exactly the same for each shot?
3. How fast or slow are you shooting (tempo)? Everyone has a "comfort" pace, study yours so you will be able to tell when you are shooting too fast or too slowly.
4. Do you load the pouch the same way for each shot?
5. Are your feet in the proper position? Are your knees straight or bent? Is your body turned?
6. Are you holding the sling at the same cant angle for each shot?
7. Is the sling oriented properly?
8. Are you breathing properly?

Show others your videotape; let them critique your stance and shooting technique. Run the tape in slow motion to better observe what you are really doing.

SELF-COACHING

Most professional athletes, like boxers, golfers, and tennis players have coaches. The coaches tell their students what to do, how to do it, and when to do it. If the student doesn't perform to the coach's standards they are disciplined in some manner or form. They pay these coaches big bucks to perform these functions so we can conclude that what they do is important. Slingshot shooting is largely an individualistic activity. We generally don't have coaches (at the present time) giving us orders and disciplining us if we don't perform properly. Since we don't employ coaches, we must take on the coaching responsibility ourselves.

In slingshots, as in any other sport, one of the coach's most important jobs is to encourage (force) the student to put in the proper "quality" practice time. Coaches use various disciplinary tactics to insure that the student practices—the self-coached shooter must also use discipline to encourage practicing. When dealing out self-discipline (punishment) some people are too hard on themselves and some people are too lenient on themselves. Each extreme can be ineffectual or even harmful. You must decide, for yourself, what type and amount of discipline is best suited for you as an individual (that's what a good coach would do).

When self-coaching, you should write down those things that the coach in you would advise you to do. Be sure to include comments on what you are doing right along with what you are doing wrong. Like any good coach your comments should never be too negative. For example, never write, "Your inconsistent stance will never allow you to become a good shooter." The statement should be "With a little discipline, you could improve your stance and consequently your accuracy." And, as a coach, you would have to recommend a treatment for the problem.

Take the job of self-coaching seriously. There are two compelling reasons for doing so: First, it will help you improve your slingshot shooting. And second, it will help you in becoming a master instructor, if you should desire, some time in the future.

TARGET PANIC

Target panic is a term used to describe an aiming problem that suddenly afflicts some experienced shooters. There are two types of target panic: Shooting before the target is acquired and the inability to bring the aim directly on the bull's-eye. The cure is to temporally use a slingshot with a very light pulling weight, bring it to full draw, and move your aim in a horizontal figure eight through the target with the bull's-eye at the intersection of the lines. Occasionally stop and hesitate with the aim on the bull's-eye. You may have to spend hours dong this exercise before you can stay on target during the hesitation. Once this is accomplished start releasing the pouch during the hesitation.

ADDRESSING BAD HABITS

At some point in our progress we inevitably develop a bad habit or two. If you have a bad habit, and are having a hard time correcting it yourself, solicit the help of your friends. For example, if you occasionally forget to breath properly, have a friend ring a bell, blow a whistle, or yell at you each time you fail to breath properly. Your shooting will suffer during the retraining process but your long-term gain will more than compensate for the short-term loss.

Minor irregularities can gradually creep into your shooting technique if you do not consciously guard against them. **Your shooting technique must be consciously examined and adjusted at the beginning of every practice session**. If you don't, an irregularity could unknowingly creep into your style for the entire practice session and become the beginning of a long-term slump.

GOOD DAYS – BAD DAYS

When practicing, you will undoubtedly have good days and bad days. When you're having a good day, stay with it because you're doing things right and staying with it will reinforce good habits. When you're having a bad day, quit practicing. You're doing something wrong and the longer you practice

121

the more you'll reinforce the bad habits. The more you reinforce bad habits, the harder they will be to correct.

On those days that you have to stop practicing, you can do other slingshot related things. Tinker with your sight, explore that slingshot modification you have been wondering about, try a new exercise, sort BBs, or do those other things that you have been putting off.

Several bad days in succession is considered to be a *"slump"*. When you're having a slump the fundamentals (basics) should be reviewed. The best way to avoid a slump is to carefully, and deliberately, **review the fundamentals each time you start a practice session**.

THE BASICS

It seems that everybody advocates, "practicing the basics" or "going back to the basics," but what are the basics? How are they unique and why are they so important? The basics are the fundamental elements that are usually done automatically.

But here is the problem: If you don't consciously think about a thing (the basics), that particular thing could gradually go astray (mutate) and you may not even be aware of it. So—the dilemma is this: The basics are good because you don't have to consciously think about them; and, the basics are troublesome because you don't consciously think about them.

We must do something to maintain the good part of the basics (frees up the conscious mind to think about aim) and eliminate the bad part (gradual degeneration). The solution is to occasionally **review the basics to renew and refresh**. Go back to the things you learned as a beginner and give them some concentrated attention.

HOW GOOD ARE YOU

How does your accuracy compare to the best shooters? When national competition started, hitting a 10-centimeter bull's-eye at 10-meters 30 percent of the time was good enough to win a tournament. Presently, it requires about 80 to 90 percent bull's-eyes to win. I expect that, in the future, shooters will become so good that they will have to increase the target distance to 20-meters, 30-meters, or even more. Even at those extended distances some dedicated competitors will hit the bull's-eye 80 percent of the time.

SLINGSHOT SHOOTING

CHAPTER 11

TOURNAMENTS

TOURNAMENT PROMOTION

What is this you say? You don't have any slingshot tournaments in your area. Well there is a sure way to fix that—promote one yourself. Pick out a suitable site, usually at an archery range, BB gun range, or pistol range. Advertise the time and location; the local newspapers may even do it for free in their "coming events" section. Take up a collection or charge a small entry fee to be used to purchase prizes. Make the prizes slingshot related (like slingshot ammo or bands) so the contestants will be motivated to stay in the sport. Be sure to coerce all your friends and relatives to attend the tournament as *seed* participants. Make sure all the participants wear safety glasses and have them sign a Liability Release form.

EQUIPMENT

Bring more than one slingshot to the tournament. You may break a band on your first slingshot in the middle of competition; there may be no time to replace a band during a match so you would have no choice but to forfeit the match. The replacement slingshot should be identical to the first slingshot.

125

In some tournaments you may be expected to shoot targets at varying distances. In one phase of the tournament you may be shooting at 10-meters and in another phase, shooting at 40-meters. In this type of tournament there are three things you can do: (1) You can simply aim higher or lower to compensate for distance. (2) You can adjust the sight on your slingshot for each distance. (If the sight can't be adjusted quickly and easily you will have to choose one of the other options.) Or (3) you can use another slingshot with the sight already set for that particular distance. Depending on the tournament structure, you may have to bring more than two or three slingshots to the tournament, each set up for a different distance.

Some power bands do not react consistently after they have been sitting idle for a time. You may spend hours setting the sights on your slingshot, and then, after it has been unused for several days, it may not be accurate when first used. Before shooting your first shot, stretch the bands three or four times to limbered them up. When not using the slingshot keep it out of the sun and try to keep the bands at a uniform temperature.

As an experiment, try this: Hold the slingshot band to your lips to feel its temperature. Then, stretch it several times, in quick succession, and again hold it to your lips. Note how much hotter it has become. The temperature change will affect its elasticity.

Be sure you use only the best BBs for tournament competition. They should be free of flat spots, scratches, and rust. If they are not from a quality vendor, be sure they are matched by size and weight.

When competing, you should wear a belt with pockets for your ammo. A modified carpenters belt can be used or, a hunter's ammo or game bag may be suitable. Make sure you are able to reach the ammo without looking at the container or changing your stance.

STRESS

Don't be surprised if you don't shoot as well in tournaments as you do in practice. The stress of emotional pressure may cause you to move your anchor point, you may be a little less steady, or you may be shooting too fast or too slowly. Be observant, determine what you are doing differently and try to correct the condition.

CHOKING

The term choking is loosely used for a variety of situations where an error is committed. As used here *choking* refers to severe anxiety that manifests itself in physical and emotional symptoms. The physical symptoms are characterized by rapid heart rate, rapid shallow breathing, upset stomach, involuntary muscle contractions, general nervousness, and clammy skin. The mind becomes overactive and tries to process input at a faster than normal speed, which prevents sustained concentration.

Psychological pressure generally does not cause choking when practicing or when in casual competition among friends. As the importance of the contest increases, psychological pressure becomes increasingly more intense which increases the chance of choking.

Few people can shoot in an important tournament without becoming emotional in some manner. Pre-tournament jitters may include fear, anxiety, butterflies in the stomach, etc. With all these emotions running rampant, your body chemistry may even change. The change in chemistry may cause you to perspire, throw up, or respond in a number of other ways.

To combat the psychological turmoil, and consequent choking, you must know when to expect the emotional turmoil, what conditions bring it on, and what the physical manifestations are. When you know what the problems are likely to be, it becomes easer to deal with them.

Don't get down on yourself if you become anxious before a big tournament. Anxiety is a natural reaction and occurs for a reason. The mind recognizes situations that require a special physical state in order to best cope with the situation. Your mind does the best it can to prepare the body for the impending task. The fact that the body is sometimes over prepared is a product of evolution. It is your job to convince your subconscious mind that the match, or tournament, is not a life or death situation.

The incapacitating effects of choking can cause a *cycle-of-frustration*. For example, choking can cause a shot to miss the bull's-eye; the frustration of missing the shot causes more anxiety, more anxiety causes more choking and around it goes. The earlier you intervene in the cycle, the easier it is to treat the symptoms.

Here are some things you can do to alleviate or minimize choking.

1. Deliberately take deep and rhythmic breaths (this helps normalize the oxygen – carbon dioxide balance in the blood).
2. Yawning occasionally will help relieve tension. We are preconditioned to associate yawning with calmness, drowsiness, or otherwise low emotional state.
3. Under stressful conditions the body produces more adrenalin (in preparation for fight or flight). Burn off the extra adrenaline by flexing your muscles. If the excess adrenalin is not burned off it will cause nervous (shaky) muscles.
4. Concentrate on the individual aspects of your task, your stance, your release, etc. Under stressful conditions the senses are all on alert, which causes them to take in too much information; deliberately narrowing your focus minimizes anxiety.
5. The human body responds to acting; for example, actors can cause the eyes to produce tears just by pretending to be sad. Pretend you are supremely confident even to the point of being arrogant.
6. Ignore your body; do not focus on any of the choking symptoms. Force yourself to focus on the elements of your shooting technique.
7. When you miss a bull's-eye, or lose a tournament, do not over-punish yourself. Anxiety is frequently caused by the fear of our own self-criticism. The more severe you punish yourself, the more anxiety you will have the next time you are in a similar situation.

8. Talk to yourself—there will be moments when you tend to relax. When this occurs, compliment yourself. The reward (compliment) will help perpetuate the relaxation.

9. Resign yourself to the fact that you are going to get nervous, learn to shoot in spite of it.

The best way to prevent choking is to treat it before any of the symptoms arise. The most important preventative action is to remain calm. Here are some things that can be done to help remain calm.

1. Meditation: Using a mantra has a calming effect. The mantra (word or phrase) is repeated over and over in the mind.

2. Pacifier: Yes, even adults can be calmed by the use of a pacifier (similar to worry beads or worry stones). Adult pacifiers are usually objects that can be rubbed, fondled, or simply looked at, for serenity.

3. Affirmations: An affirmation is a positive statement or judgment. The theory is that repeating an affirmation over and over will cause it to be embedded in the mind and the person repeating the affirmation will think and act in a desired manner. Affirmations are also referred to as self-talk, clichés, proclamations, assertions, truisms, and platitudes. Call them whatever you like, they work (at least for most people).

4. Self analysis: Human beings are highly individualistic, what helps you may not help someone else. Observe yourself, when you do or say something that helps you remain calm, jot it down for future reference.

Consider this: To help desensitize yourself to anxiety, deliberately shoot in the biggest most stressful tournament you can find. After that experience you can tell yourself that there is no reason for anxiety because you have experienced the worst.

Some people cause themselves to choke by overemphasizing the importance of winning. To reduce this tendency, priorities must be shifted. Instead of making winning your first priority, make staying calm your first priority. Just saying that you're shifting priorities doesn't make it so. In fact, there is a compelling tendency to say it just so you can win. To actually shift priorities you must be prepared to lose a few tournaments in the process. Eventually, remaining calm will become easier and shooting higher scores will happen even with the lowered priority.

MENTAL PREPAREDNESS

Right-brain – left-brain -- The human brain consists of two hemispheres separated in the vertical plane. Each hemisphere operates in a specific manner and performs specific functions. Data is stored in the left-brain in objective form such as words, numbers, etc. These data are processed in a logical sequential manner like in a computer. The right-brain stores, retrieves, and processes subjective information. The subjective information is in the form of sounds, smells, tastes, images, and emotions. The right-brain

131

does not understand language, it cannot comprehend words, numbers etc.

When you are preparing to shoot in a tournament, it is important to alert both the left- and right-brain about the impending task. Alerting the left-brain is no problem because it understands language and it knows all about the tournament. The right-brain doesn't understand language so it is difficult to inform it of the imminent challenge. However, the right-brain does understand visual, auditory, and tactile stimuli, so these senses have to be used to inform it of the upcoming task. Rituals that involve the senses can be used to communicate with the right-brain. For example, wear your lucky green socks when you shoot in tournaments, the green socks will alert your right-brain as to the pending task (tournament). Be sure to use the green socks only for tournaments. If you use them for any other occasion you won't be sending a clear, concise, message to the brain and its purpose will be defeated.

Did you notice that this type of ritual is very similar to a superstition? Perhaps you have heard of tennis players wearing their "lucky head band" for the big tournament or the boxer wearing his "lucky trunks" for the championship bout. They may think they are wearing those things as a superstition, what they are actually doing is cueing their right-brain as to the importance of the task ahead.

Imaging -- Imaging must be used on a large scale, which encompasses the entire tournament, including the final result. The ability to imagine, or actually picture, the end result of your actions takes away the anxiety and builds confidence. Imagine your victory, in detail, prior to the tournament. Imagine all the positive emotions that you will feel when you win the tournament. Imagine the joy and adulation of your friends when you win. Imagine all of these things as though they have already happened. This process helps program the right-brain as to the desired final result.

Rehearsals -- In any sport or competition, participants must prepare to win by rehearsing the image of winning. Rehearsing being a winner should be done in great detail and at great length. Know exactly what you are going to say, know exactly what you will do and the sequence in which you will do things. Pretend you are a movie director. Dictate every minute detail from the dialog, to the action, to the emotion. After all this rehearsing, winning will no longer be a strange unknown situation plagued with anxieties. Your subconscious mind will no longer keep you from winning because there will be no fear of the unknown.

PHYSICAL PREPAREDNESS

Muscle tension -- Occasionally, walking can alleviate a mild case of muscle tension. Take a stroll before showing up for the tournament; a short walk to the restroom can be relaxing. Even abbreviated movement such as fidgeting can be beneficial. Repeatedly fidget with your equipment, your cloths, and your ammo.

Warm up -- A stretching routine is recommended before you step to the line to shoot your first shot. When warming up be sure to include the circular exercise routine and the pulling routine that you have been doing with your arms. Don't over stress the shooting muscles; exercise with only about a quarter of the weight you normally use.

Rest and relaxation -- When shooting in a tournament you should strive to get your normal amount of sleep the night before the big event. More, or less, than the normal amount may be detrimental to your efficiency.

It takes some time after awakening before all the muscles begin to function at peak efficiency. You should allow a minimum of two hours between waking and competitive shooting. Walking or other mild form of exercise helps to stimulate muscle coordination.

The eyes should be rested prior to the big event. Avoid reading, television, bright lighting, and even driving if possible.

Eating -- All serious athletes should have a regimented diet and eating schedule prior to the big tournament. Anxiety causes the stomach to constrict and produce excess acid. If too much food is eaten, anxiety may cause the stomach to throw it back up. Even a mild case of stomach upset can be distracting and may trigger a cycle-of-frustration. Before the big event, eat only light, easily digestible food—this means carbohydrates like fruits and vegetables. Avoid fat and protein, this means **<u>no</u>** hamburgers or hot dogs.

SPONSORSHIP

One of the most important things in perpetuating professional sports is sponsorship money. Events are sponsored and players are sponsored. Without sponsorship money most professional sports would fail.

Events -- Everyone knows that big time sporting events have big time corporate sponsorship. They contribute by purchasing signage and paying for advertising. The money they contribute goes toward organizing the tournament, paying prize money, and many other things. This type of sponsorship system does not have to be confined only to big events. The same motivational forces exist regardless of the size of the event. Local tournament promoters should seek out sponsorship even though it may be on a small scale.

Participants -- Not everyone can be a world-class shooter, but most shooters can be at the top of some smaller venue. That is, you could be the top shooter in your company, your block, or your zip code. Even if you are not an expert slingshot shooter you can still solicit sponsorship. Solicit the local sports bars, sporting supply stores, grocery stores, and all the other businesses in the area. Sponsorship does not have to be based on a long formal contract when you are operating at the lower levels. For example, you could wear a sponsor's shirt in return for all or part of your entrance fee. Be sure to insist that the tournament director mentions your sponsor's name when referring to you. Don't be embarrassed by starting small, the better you become, the more attractive you will be to the larger sponsors. By starting early, and small, you will be getting good experience as well as exposure. As your skills progress, and you enter bigger and bigger tournaments, you can become more selective about whose products you endorse.

If you dress well, speak well, and act well, you should be able to obtain sponsorship at some level. Sponsors don't like to take a chance; if they think there is a chance that you will do something embarrassing, they cannot, and will not, take a chance on you. No sponsor wants to be represented by someone that may get caught taking dope or doing some other dumb or illegal thing. When you participate in a tournament, you are a reflection of your sponsor; if you embarrass yourself, you embarrass your sponsor.

Sponsorship may even encourage you to shoot better than you would otherwise shoot. Look around; if you are the only person that is being sponsored, you have a psychological edge.

We should all feel a responsibility to cater to vendors that sponsor tournaments and individuals. In doing so we encourage additional sponsorship and subsequent growth of our sport.

SLINGSHOT SHOOTING

CHAPTER 12

HUNTING

SMALL GAME

So, what can you hunt with a slingshot? Practically any small animals like squirrels, rabbits, grouse and pheasants are potential game. Sparrows, starlings, and crows are tempting targets around the farm. Little varmints like mice, rats, and snakes are also challenging targets. It can even be fun to hunt bees and hornets using sand as ammunition. Animals as large as a coyote have reportedly been killed with a slingshot. However, for every large animal killed many more will be only harmed or maimed in the process of trying to harvest a large trophy. Do **not** try to see how large an animal you can kill.

If you are going to hunt living things, be humane. Take only good clean killing shots, generally a head shot is required to kill instantaneously. Shoot only at close range; hone your stalking skills so that you can get very close to your target before taking a shot.

Rabbits and pheasants occasionally are easy targets because they often "hold tight" which allows a slingshot hunter to approach within several feet before they run or fly away. In some areas, especially in the northern United States, various types of grouse are plentiful and will also freeze in position offering a good chance at a headshot.

139

SLINGSHOT SHOOTING

Even fish can be hunted with a slingshot. However, shooting fish requires a special type of slingshot designed specifically to shoot barbed arrows. The arrows are generally attached to a fishing line so the fish can be retrieved.

BIG GAME

When I was a young man I use to hunt deer every year (with a rifle). The excitement of the approaching deer season seemed to overwhelm all other activities. It was always difficult to sleep the night before opening day. The joy of being out in the elements deer hunting suppressed even the nastiest cold wintry weather conditions. This went on for many years. But for some reason, I started to lose the urge to hunt. It was not so much that I didn't want to hunt, it was the fact that I didn't want to kill the dear. It got to a point that I could not pull the trigger—so, I quit hunting deer. Although I had quit hunting, I still had the yearning for the stealth and stalk.

Many years past, then one day I had an epiphany: I would hunt dear with my slingshot—but with a twist. I would use paintballs instead of slugs for ammunition. This would satisfy my urge for stalking. Having to get close to the deer, in order to take a shot, made the stalk even more challenging. The fact that there were deer running around in the woods with my paint mark on them (if only for a few days) was all the reward I needed for my effort.

I use much the same hunting techniques bow hunters use; I hunt from tree stands and much more challenging, from camouflaged ground stands. For me, this type of hunting has all the good stuff and none of the bad stuff. I hate dragging a dead deer's carcass out of the woods, I hate gutting and skinning, and I hate all that butchering stuff. Another advantage of using a slingshot and paint balls is that I can shoot the deer in any part of their anatomy, including in the hindquarters, and I won't ruin any meat. As it turns out, I now enjoy hunting deer more than ever before. If the opportunity ever comes up, I would like to try my luck at bear hunting. If you enjoy hunting big game, but not necessarily the killing, slingshot hunting is for you.

Serious bow hunters can also make good use of the slingshot. When posting in a tree stand it is not unusual to have more does and fawns congregating at your bait station than bucks. If you are insistent on only harvesting a buck, you can chase the does away with a well-placed paint-ball shot. Or, you can shoot them with a paint ball simply out of frustration.

DISTANCE VARIABLES

If you practice target shooting at a distance of 10-meters you can become very accurate at that specific distance. However, when hunting, the distance to the target will vary. You can use 10-meters as your reference distance and aim higher, if the target is farther away, and aim lower if it is closer. Shooting up (like into a tree) or down also requires an aim adjustment.

It is advisable that you practice estimating distances, and shooting at various distances, before doing any serious hunting. Using a sight, on your slingshot, is fine for target shooting but most shooters believe that it is better to use instinctive aiming when hunting. This aiming technique automatically adjusts for distance. Practice the instinctive aiming technique when you're walking in the woods. Pick out a knot on a tree, estimate the distance and take a shot, move closer or farther away and try another shot. Eventually you will be ready to do some serious hunting.

> I like to create my own targets in the woods. I shoot at a tree or stump with a paint ball. The paint mark makes a perfect target.

If your hunting technique requires that you sit-in-wait (posting) for your prey to appear at a specific spot (by a rabbit trail for example); it is advisable to take a few shots at the place where you expect the game to appear. This way you can make the aiming adjustment before shooting at the varmint. If there are several places where the game is likely to appear, take a few shots at all of them. (Gun hunters can't do that because the noise would scare off their intended targets.)

EQUIPMENT

Power bands -- Average slingshots with average bands are excellent for target shooting and plinking. However, for hunting, the bands should be a little stronger. Where the average band may have a 10- to 20-pound pull at full draw, the hunting band should ideally have a 20- to 30-pound pull. In any case, use the strongest bands you can find because they can accommodate a larger BB (especially if $\frac{1}{2}$-inch, or larger, BBs are being used). If your slingshot has a draw-length adjustment, set it at the longest draw available. If you make your own hunting slingshot, it may be advisable to put two bands on each side to help accommodate the larger ammo.

Note: If a mechanical sight is used, it must be set for the specific band force and ammunition that you are using. If several different sizes of ammo are being used, with the same slingshot, the sight should have a specific mark for each size BB.

Ammunition -- The projectile size and weight must be appropriate for the game you are hunting. Larger, heaver steel BBs ($\frac{1}{2}$-inch or more in diameter) are generally used for larger game like rabbits or pheasants. A faster $\frac{3}{8}$-inch steel BB is better suited for smaller animals like rats and mice. Remember, the shot does not normally kill by penetration and bleeding, it kills by blunt-force trauma. Therefore, the heaver the projectile, the more stopping power it will have.

For some, lead balls (high density) are favored for hunting because of their high knockout punch. However, because of environmental considerations it is much better to use steel balls.

When hunting, ammunition should be kept in an easily accessible pouch or pocket. A carpenter's belt with several pockets is ideal. You should be able to reach into a pocket and get the proper size BB without looking. If you take your eyes off a squirrel, as it is running from branch to branch, you will probably lose sight of it.

SAFETY

It is always uncomfortable to wear safety glasses and doubly so when hunting. But regardless of the discomfort, it is always advisable to wear safety glasses when hunting. The sooner you resign yourself to wearing glasses, the sooner the glasses will become part of your accepted equipment.

When target shooting, the conditions and environment are controlled to a large degree. When hunting, things are not so well controlled. Always be aware of the direction you are shooting. Are there any other hunters, farm animals, or buildings in your shooting direction? Shooting into rock piles can be dangerous because of ricochet BBs. Shooting at birds or squirrels in trees is dangerous because the BBs will travel a long distance if the target is missed.

LEGAL CONSIDERATIONS

Most areas do not require a slingshot to be registered. They generally aren't considered to be a weapon and therefore no special handling permits are required. But, if you use your slingshot for hunting, you'll likely still be required to have a hunting license. Be cautioned, in some areas, it is illegal to hunt any type of game with a slingshot. It is recommended that you check with your local game warden if you are going to harvest animals. Never hunt, even with paint balls, until you know the local laws. Call the local authorities, or better yet, write to them (this way you have a written record) before you go into the woods with your slingshot.

SLINGSHOT SHOOTING

CHAPTER 13

EPILOGUE

Having read this book, you have gained a good start with regard to basic slingshot knowledge, but don't stop here. Introduce your friends and relatives to the sport—some of them will fall in love with slingshots and will be forever grateful to you. Share your knowledge about slingshots; half the pleasure of having knowledge is being able to share it with others. Tell your friends and colleagues that you're a slingshot shooter; let them know you have a unique talent.

Some people associate slingshots with little mischievous boys; therefore, there may be some snickers when you tell them you have an interest in slingshots. If that is the case, tell them about me; I'm sixty-nine years old and my passion for slingshots is growing with each passing year.

Get your friends involved in slingshot shooting—invite them over for a slingshot shoot-out. Be sure to have a few extra slingshots and safety glasses for them to use.

When you shoot your personal best, you get a feeling of satisfaction that is difficult to describe. Although the feeling is difficult to describe, all of us shooters know exactly what you feel because we have all felt the same emotions. Knowing we share these emotions is one of life's most gratifying experiences.

147

SLINGSHOT SHOOTING

Always conduct yourself with courtesy and sportsmanship; your actions will reflect on the sport as well as on yourself as an individual. Go forth as a standard bearer, do your part to promote and popularize the sport. The future of slingshot shooting depends on people like you; join me in helping to take the sport to the highest level possible.

ABOUT
AUTHOR

I am sixty-nine years old (that's an old picture) and have had a passion for slingshots all my life. When I was a kid, I was rarely without my trusty slingshot. Whether I was sent out to bring the cows home for evening milking or going over to the neighbors for a dozen eggs, I always had my beloved slingshot with me. I couldn't walk in the woods without scanning the trees looking for a suitable fork to make yet another slingshot (I find myself still doing that). I couldn't walk down a road without

149

constantly scanning for round stones suitable for ammunition (all the local roads were gravel at that time).

I love the shooting sports. I have several rifles, shotguns, and pistols but rarely do I ever shoot any of them. My slingshots are another story; I now practice target shooting, with my slingshots, at every opportunity. During the middle part of my life I went many years without shooting a slingshot because of other interest (pocket billiards) and obligations. Looking back, I regret not making room in my life for slingshot shooting during that period.

By profession I was a Hydrologist. I spent my entire career working for the U.S. Geological Survey. During that time I authored twenty-five Professional Papers. After retiring, I wrote three very successful books on pocket billiards.

NOTES

EQUIPMENT PURCHASE
OR MODIFICATION

Date	Item	Description	Evaluation

NOTES

BAND CHARACTERISTICS

Date	Description and dimensions	Pull force	Projectile velocity

NOTES

IMPORTANT CONTACTS

Name	Phone--address or email	Significants

NOTES

SLINGSHOT EVENTS

Date	Event	Evaluation

STANCE AND STYLE
EXPERIMENTS

Date	Description of change	Evaluation

NOTES

SCORES TO REMEMBER

Date	Target	Distance	Description